EVERYTHING
YOU NEED TO KNOW ABOUT...

Digital
Photography

EVERYTHING

YOU NEED TO KNOW ABOUT...

Digital Photography

ELIZABETH T. SCHOCH

David & Charles

A DAVID & CHARLES BOOK

David & Charles is a subsidiary of F+W (UK) Ltd.,

an F+W Publications Inc. company

First published in the UK in 2004

First published in the USA as The Everything® Digital Photography Book,

by Adams Media Corporation in 2002

Project Manager Ian Kearey

Cover Design Ali Myer

A catalogue record for this book is available from the British Library.

ISBN 0 7153 2063 7

Printed in Great Britain by CPI Bath

for David & Charles

Brunel House   Newton Abbot   Devon

Visit our website at www.davidandcharles.co.uk

David & Charles books are available from all good bookshops;

alternatively you can contact our Orderline on (0)1626 334555

or write to us at FREEPOST EX2110, David & Charles Direct,

Newton Abbot, TQ12 4ZZ (no stamp required UK mainland).

Contents

Introduction ix

**CHAPTER 1 What's So Great About
Digital Photography?. 1**
Photography Then and Now 2
The Digital Debate. 7
The Benefits of Going Digital 9
The Other Side of the Coin. 11
From SLR to Digital 12
Commercial Uses for Digital Photography. . . . 13
Is Digital for You? 14

**CHAPTER 2 Understanding How
Cameras Work 15**
How Digital Cameras Work 16
Colour Your World Digital 18
Image Resolution and Image Quality 18
Determining the Number of Pixels
You Need 21
Keeping the Right Size 22
Adjusting Pixels and Resolution 22
Overview of Resolution. 24

**CHAPTER 3 What to Look For in a
Digital Camera 27**
Finding a Camera to Meet Your Needs. 28
Checklist of Secondary Features. 32
What You Can Expect to Spend. 32
Cameras for Special Needs 34

**CHAPTER 4 Buying the Digital Camera That's Right
for You 37**
A Step-by-Step Guide 38
Investigating the Choices 39

Going, Going, Gone – Buying
at Online Auctions 42
Is It Time to Buy? 43
Looking After a Digital Camera. 44

CHAPTER 5 Image Sensors 47
CCD Versus CMOS. 48
Image Sensor Resolution 50
Aspect Ratio 50
Colour Depth. 51
Frame Rate. 51
Sensitivity 52
Image Quality. 53

CHAPTER 6 Image Storage (Memory). 55
Removable Memory Versus Fixed Storage. . . . 56
Flash Memory Cards 57
Memory Card Adapters. 59
Caring for Your Memory Cards 61

CHAPTER 7 Lenses 63
Focal Length 64
Determining Focal Length 65
Maximum Aperture 66
Focusing Methods. 66
Types of Lenses. 68
Taking a Closer Look
at Macro Photography 71
Lens Accessories 72
Evaluating a Lens. 73

CHAPTER 8 Flash. 75
Limitations. 76
Settings 76
Additional Light Sources. 79
Shooting at Night 82

CHAPTER 9 Batteries, LCD Screens
and Viewfinders **83**
Alkaline Batteries 84
Choosing Rechargeable Batteries 84
Battery Chargers 86
Getting the Most From Your Batteries 87
Buying Batteries on the Web 88
LCD Screens 89
Viewfinders 91

CHAPTER 10 Creative Controls
and Other Features **93**
Creative Controls 94
Autoexposure 94
Metering Systems 95
Exposure Compensation 96
Aperture Priority and Shutter Priority Modes 97
Autoflash 98
Autofocus 98
Adjusting Colour Balance 99
Continuous Mode 100
Panoramic Mode 101
Self-Timers/Remote Controls 102

CHAPTER 11 What Makes a Photograph
Memorable **103**
Shape 104
Line 104
Pattern 106
Texture 108
Composition 109
Angle of View 112
Framing 113
Colour 113
Light 114

CHAPTER 12 Taking Great Pictures **119**
Getting Ready to Shoot 120
Taking the Picture 121

Time and Its Effect on Photographs 126

CHAPTER 13 Types of Photographs **129**
Portraits 130
Candids 131
Pets 132
Landscapes 133
Still Lifes 136
Silhouettes 138
Cities 138
Architectural Details 140
Close-Ups 141
Good Pictures Are Everywhere 142
Photography Log 143

CHAPTER 14 Downloading Images **145**
Connecting Your Camera With Cable 146
Downloading Directly From Storage Media . 149
Wireless Transfers 151
Other Types of Transfers 153

CHAPTER 15 Image Compression
and File Formats **155**
How Compression Works 156
Lossy Versus Lossless Compression 156
File Formats 157
Compression (Archive) Formats 162

CHAPTER 16 Storing Your
Digital Images **165**
Understanding Computer Memory 166
Saving Your Images 166
What's in a Name? 171

CHAPTER 17 Scanners **173**
What Is a Scanner and
Why Do I Need One? 174
Flatbed Scanners 175
Film Scanners 176

Combination Scanners 177
Drum Scanners 178
Handheld Scanners. 178
Small-Footprint Scanners 179
Are More Bits Necessarily Better? 180
Which Scanner Is Right for You? 181
Handy Tools 186
Where Do Your Scans Go? 186
Tips for Good Scanning 187

CHAPTER 18 Printers. 189
The Printing Process 190
Inkjet Printers. 190
Dye Sublimation Printers 191
Thermo-Autochrome Printers 192
Solid Inkjet Printers 192
Colour Laser Printers 193
Making Your Choice. 193
Types of Printing 194
Printers and Resolution. 195
Using the Right Type of Paper 197
How Long Can I Expect
    My Prints to Last? 198

**CHAPTER 19 Improving Your
        Digital Pictures. 199**
Ways to Improve Your Digital
    Images While Shooting 200
Creating Your Digital Darkroom. 202
Choosing an Image Editor. 202
Overview of Imaging Tools 205
Image-Editing Tips. 206
The Power of Editing Tools 208
Correcting Your Digital Images 208

**CHAPTER 20 Getting Creative
        With Digital Images 213**
Replacing the Traditional Darkroom. 214
Camera-like Results. 216

Artistic Effects 217
Special Effects 218
Having Fun With Your Photos 222
Digital Photographs: Other Good Uses. 224

**CHAPTER 21 Image-Editing
        Software 227**
Overview of Image-Editing Programs. 228
Questions to Ask When Choosing
    Consumer-Level Software 228
Advanced Image-Editing
    Software Programs 230
Intermediate Programs. 232
Beginner Programs 234

CHAPTER 22 Using the Web. 237
Taking Your Images Online 238

APPENDIX A Glossary 243

APPENDIX B Resources 251
Camera Manufacturer Websites 251
Scanner Manufacturer Websites 252

Index 253

Introduction

We are living in a digital world. From compact discs to mobile phones to MP3s to computers, we use digital technology every day to enjoy music, to communicate with others and to access information via the Internet. Even televisions boast digital technology. It's not surprising, then, that photography, too, has gone digital in a big way.

What would our grandparents have thought if they'd been told that one day photographers would be able to take photographs without the use of film? Surely it would have sounded like science fiction, but that day is here, and an increasing number of photographers – both amateur and professional – are embracing the technology that allows images to be captured and stored digitally. In 1999, worldwide shipment of digital cameras exceeded 6.5 million units, according to Digital Camera Market Forecast and Analysis from International Data Group, a provider of industry analysis and market data. That number was expected to jump dramatically to 41.6 million units by the end of 2004.

Here are some of the reasons why photographers are choosing to go digital:

·   No film is needed
·   It saves time and money
·   There is no more darkroom (it is replaced by your computer)
·   It offers a quick way to check your photos
·   It provides an easy way to obtain an image for a webpage

Digital cameras offer photographers many benefits, but two compelling reasons typically sway people to make the switch to digital from film (analogue) cameras:

·   The freedom to manipulate the output (digital image)
·   The instant gratification that comes from being able to access the results immediately.

With new digital cameras and countless new options popping up every day, millions of people are discovering the joys of digital photography.

In 2003, sales of digital cameras outstripped those of film cameras. Even people who never thought of themselves as photographers are getting on the digital camera bandwagon. Why? Because this is one piece of high-tech equipment that is actually fun to use!

How many times have you been walking down the street, visiting relatives or playing with your kids when you have seen something or someone and thought, 'That would make a great picture'? A digital camera means you'll never again miss that wonderful shot.

Once you're hooked on digital photography, you won't want to leave your camera at home, and thanks to its portability, you won't have to. Because a digital camera can be compact and lightweight, it's easy to carry in your pocket or purse. And since it doesn't need film, there's no need to worry about whether it's loaded. You're always ready to capture the moment, so you can grab it and start snapping away.

After you've taken that once-in-a-lifetime shot, it's easy to download it to your computer and send it off via e-mail to loved ones near and far. Part of the beauty of digital photography is the ease of sharing photos. It's fun to take digital photos, and it's even more fun to share them with others.

With so many British households owning personal computers, it's no wonder that people are embracing digital photography instead of, or in addition to, their traditional cameras. They're finding that it's easy to download digital photos into a PC, and it's great fun to become really creative, using software to modify a picture, then zapping it onto the Internet for others to experience. Faster and more sophisticated software programs are continuously appearing in high-street shops, making the options for modifying digital images almost limitless.

The bottom line, then, appears to be this: digital photography provides a new and exciting way for ordinary people to express their creativity. It also offers them a means to communicate with friends, relatives and business associates, anywhere from the next street to more than half a world away.

CHAPTER 1

What's So Great About Digital Photography?

efore digital cameras, the only way to get a digital image was to take a picture with a film camera, get the film developed, then have the photographic print or slide digitized using a scanner. Digital cameras eliminate the time needed for developing and scanning. When you own a digital camera, you can miss out the darkroom and go straight to the desktop.

Photography Then and Now

Before we consider digital photography more closely, let's pause and take a look back at photography's roots.

The term 'photography' was first coined by the scientist Sir John Herschel in 1839. The word is derived from the Greek words *photos* (light) and *graphein* (to draw). Two scientific processes, one optical and the other chemical, combined to make photography possible. Interestingly, both processes had existed for hundreds of years before photography was invented.

The Optical Process: Using Light to Create Images

The equipment that became the foundation for modern photography was nothing like today's cameras. The forerunners of modern cameras were created from darkened rooms. Light came in through a small hole in the room's window shade or wall, causing an upside-down image of what was outside to appear on the opposite wall. This device was called a camera obscura, which means 'dark chamber' in Latin.

The concept of the camera obscura has been around for thousands of years. It is believed that the great Greek philosopher Aristotle (384–322 BCE) knew the principle behind the camera obscura, as did the Arabian scholar Hassan bin Hassan, who in the 10th century described in his manuscripts something that can be considered a camera obscura.

Later, Leonardo da Vinci (1452–1519) wrote about the uses of a camera obscura and depicted one in a drawing dated 1519. During the same period, a Venetian named Daniel Barbaro recommended that the camera obscura be used as an aid to drawing and perspective. And in 1558, Giovanni Battista della Porta wrote a book called *Natural Magic* that told of the camera obscura being utilized as a tool by draughtsmen and illustrators. From that time onwards, it is thought that many artists employed the camera obscura, including the Dutch artist Johannes Vermeer (1632–75) and the British artists Joshua Reynolds (1723–92), first president of the Royal Academy of Art in London, and Paul Sandby (1725–1809), a founding member of the Royal Academy.

As time went by, the camera obscura grew smaller in size. Made from a wooden box, it had a lens attached at one end and a mirror at the other. The mirror was positioned at a 45-degree angle, with a glass plate above it. By placing a piece of thin paper over the glass, an individual could trace the image projected there.

In 1949, the American Gene Turtle built a camera obscura as part of a thesis project. The Giant Camera, formerly part of an amusement park in San Francisco, remains standing in California today. Visitors find that once they step inside, they see the same views they'd see outside — but in much greater detail than can be seen in daylight.

The Chemical Process: Bringing Images to Paper

In the 17th century, Robert Boyle, a chemist and co-founder of the Royal Society, reported that silver chloride turned dark under exposure, but he mistakenly believed that it was exposure to air – rather than exposure to light – that caused this to happen.

During the 1700s and 1800s, several people were experimenting with photosensitive materials. One of these, a German physicist named Johann Heinrich Schulze, discovered in 1727 that light could be used to change substances. He experimented with silver, nitric acid and chalk, and found that bright sunlight turned the mixture to black. Although his discovery, in conjunction with the camera obscura, provided the basic technology for photography, it was not until the 19th century that photography came into being.

In the early 1800s, Frenchman Joseph Niepce discovered that exposing bitumen, an asphalt-like substance, to light caused it to harden. He coated metal plates with bitumen, then exposed them to light inside a camera obscura. After an exposure of eight hours, the plate was washed and dipped in acid, which etched the exposed metal. The last step was to coat the plate with ink and strike it on paper, producing a print of the original image. Niepce named this process heliography, and he is regarded as having produced the first permanent photographic image.

At about the same time that Niepce developed heliography, another Frenchman, Louis Daguerre, a successful commercial artist, was experimenting with the same process. Niepce and Daguerre formed a partnership in 1829, but Niepce died a few years later. Daguerre continued to experiment by coating a copper plate with silver, then exposing the silver to iodine fumes, creating a silver-iodide salt that made the plate photosensitive. He put the plate in the camera obscura and exposed it to light. The silver-iodide darkened, but eventually the entire image turned black.

Quite by accident, Daguerre found a solution to his dilemma. One day he left an exposed plate in a cabinet where mercury was stored. When he removed the plate, he realized that the developing had ceased and the image had stopped darkening. He named his invention the daguerreotype. When Louis Daguerre showed the first daguerreotypes to the public in the winter of 1838–39, Parisians were amazed by the amount of detail they contained. Some likened looking through a magnifying glass at a daguerreotype to viewing nature through a telescope. Daguerre's English rival for the title of inventor of modern photography, William Henry Fox Talbot, had this to say about the detail of a daguerreotype:

> It frequently happens, moreover – and this is one of the charms of photography – that the operator himself discovers on examination, perhaps long afterwards, that he has depicted many things he had no notion of at the time. Sometimes inscriptions and dates are found upon the buildings, or printed placards most irrelevant are discovered upon their walls; sometimes a distant dial-plate is seen, and upon it – unconsciously recorded – the hour of the day at which the view was taken.

At about the same time that Daguerre was developing the daguerreotype, Fox Talbot was experimenting with a similar process. However, Talbot used paper instead of metal plates and produced a 'negative' image. He then took the paper negative, waxed it to make it translucent and photographed it to produce a 'positive' image. He called the resulting positive-negative image a calotype. Talbot is sometimes hailed as the father of modern photography, since the basis of the process he developed is used in photography today, but unquestionably Daguerre was an equally essential contributor to the development of photography.

The Female Perspective

Although the originators of modern photography were mostly men, women were also experimenting with the photographic process during the 19th century. Even as William Henry Fox Talbot was developing the positive-negative process, his wife was conducting her own experiments, which she detailed in writing in 1839.

Women were attracted to photography because in the 19th and early 20th centuries it was one of the few professions deemed acceptable for their participation. There were also many women enjoying photography as a hobby. Camera clubs were formed, and various art salons began to exhibit the work of amateur women photographers.

One notable English female photographer was Julia Margaret Cameron (1815–79), known for her portraits of eminent people and for her romantic pictures which, despite their technical imperfections, stand the test of time. Her involvement in photography came about when she was 49: her children had grown up, and her husband was often abroad on business. Her daughter bought her a camera to give her something to do. From this simple beginning a new hobby began, which was to turn into an obsession. Cameron had a tremendous capacity to visualize a picture, and her portraits have a great measure of vitality. Among her most famous portraits are those of Herschel and Tennyson. She was greatly appreciated in Europe and the USA, and won a number of major prizes.

Although histories of photography have a tendency to focus on the men who were pioneers in the field, it is timely to remember that women played a part in its early days.

Daguerreotypes' Popularity Spreads

Daguerre's process spread throughout the world, with the first daguerreotypes being made in England in 1839. At first the process of creating an exposure was quite lengthy. Moving objects could not be recorded, and it was difficult to obtain portraits because of the lengthy exposure time required.

Individuals in Britain, mainland Europe and the USA began experimenting to improve the optical, chemical and practical aspects of the daguerreotype process to make it more workable for creating portraits. In 1840 Alexander Wolcott opened a 'daguerrean parlour' in New York, where he created tiny portraits using a camera fitted with a mirror instead of a lens. Wolcott's daguerrean parlour was the world's earliest known photography studio.

Jozsef Petzval and Friedrich Voigtlander, both of Vienna, revolutionized the daguerreotype process. Petzval produced a portrait lens that was about 20 times faster than had been previously used, and Voigtlander reconstructed Daguerre's wooden box into one that was smaller and easier to transport. At about the same time, Franz Kratochwilz, also from Vienna, developed and published a chemical acceleration process that increased the sensitivity of the developing plate. With these valuable improvements, exposure time was reduced to 20–40 seconds, and daguerreotyping became a flourishing business.

Eastman Instrumental in Modern Photography

In the latter part of the 1800s, the American George Eastman advanced the photographic process to such an extent that his influence is still felt today. In 1879 he invented an emulsion-coating machine that enabled the mass production of photographic dry plates, and in 1880 he began to manufacture them. In the early 1880s Eastman began experimenting with emulsion-support bases made of other materials than glass. Working with a colleague, he developed a roll-film holder, a flexible film and a machine to produce the film. They layered the film with gelatin emulsions on a paper backing, then stripped off the backing after development.

By 1885 Eastman American Film, the first transparent film negative, was introduced. Three years later Kodak was born, and the Kodak camera was introduced. The camera, which sold for $25 (£16), came loaded with 100 exposures on a film roll. Once all the film had been used up, the camera was sent back to the Eastman Dry Plate and Film Co. in Rochester, New York, for developing. One year later, Kodak No. 2, the first commercial transparent roll film, was launched on the market.

The Eastman Dry Plate and Film Co. became the Eastman Company in 1889, and then Eastman Kodak Company of New York in 1892. In 1895 the Pocket Kodak Camera was announced, followed in 1900 by the first mass-marketed camera, the Brownie, which sold for $1 (13/- or 65p). With its wide availability and affordable price, the Brownie camera allowed all but the very poor to take up photography. This was the beginning of the 20th century's love affair with the snapshot.

The development of Kodak No. 2 flexible film made it possible for Thomas Edison to develop the motion picture camera in 1891.

The Digital Debate

Which are better: traditional film (analogue) cameras or digital cameras? This issue is hotly debated, and it appears that a definitive answer will remain elusive for some time. Depending on who you talk to, digital cameras seem like the be-all and end-all, and everyone who is anyone is rushing out to buy one. But there are also traditional photographers who are quick to maintain that the quality of photographs produced by digital cameras cannot match the quality provided by a film camera, at least not for the same price. In a nutshell, these are some of the specific points that cause debate:

·   Are digital prints as good as 35mm prints? Some people think that digital prints are actually better. With a 2-megapixel camera, digital prints can rival 35mm prints in quality. Working with a good printer, you can produce astounding images.
·   The ability to edit as you go is one of the main advantages of digital cameras. Rather than having to wade through poor shots and discard them, you can quickly delete any bad ones from your camera, leaving only the best in the memory.
·   Digital is fun. There's something tremendously appealing about using a digital camera. It's partly the instant gratification that comes from being able to upload your memory card immediately after a shoot. It's

also knowing that you can effortlessly share your pictures with anyone, anywhere, thanks to the Internet and e-mail. Free photo-sharing websites also make it enjoyable and easy to share photos using online albums.

·   The chance to have some creative recreation with your photos using a software program is another strong draw of digital photography. With the help of your computer, you can enhance your photos in a million different ways, or you can make greetings cards, enhance personal or business newsletters or add sparkle and originality to your website.

Now for the opposite side:

·   Film is available everywhere; memory cards are not. If you're travelling far from home, it may not be as easy to pick up more memory cards as it would be to buy more film. And it's certainly not as cheap – you can't just pop into a corner shop to stock up on memory cards. If you are travelling to a remote area, you're unlikely to find xD Picture-Cards or CompactFlash available if you need them. Instead, you will need to make a rather substantial investment in memory before you even leave home.

·   Many photographers believe that film still offers better resolution than digital images.

·   Digital cameras run into problems when they are used to shoot in low-light locations. Film offers greater sensitivity to light, allowing the photographer a greater chance of getting a good shot in low light. With your digital camera, you may need to add extra sources of light in order to get a good photo.

When travelling, you can amass an unlimited number of rolls of film. With a digital camera, you either have to stop and download your images to a computer, or you must have a large number of digital memory cards with you – requiring not only a lot of planning ahead but also a sizeable financial investment.

- Digital cameras run into parallax problems more frequently than film models. (See Chapter 9 for more on parallax problems.)
- There are more lenses available for 35mm cameras. Fewer lenses mean fewer ways to be creative with your camera.
- Film cameras provide quicker shutter response than digital cameras, resulting in better sports and action shots.

The Benefits of Going Digital

Not everyone needs, or wants, a digital camera. If you are satisfied with your film camera, you may not want to purchase a digital camera. This is especially true if you do not own a computer and are not planning to purchase one soon, or at all. But there are some distinct advantages to digital photography, which you should consider before making your decision. Many find that it pays to have both a 35mm SLR camera and a digital camera. Here's why digital photography is so appealing:

- *It's the wave of the future.* Using a digital camera means working with cutting-edge photography. About every three or four weeks, a new model digital camera makes its appearance on the market. And digital cameras' capabilities are expanding at what seems like the speed of light. In fact, remarkable audio- and video-machines are being manufactured. For instance, you can now enjoy multifunction digital cameras, such as Fujifilm's FinePix 40I, which shoots digital stills, records MP3 audio and takes digital video with sound – although not all at the same time. But even if you are not in the market for a camera that sophisticated, you may still be eager to explore the digital world for the advantages it offers.
- *No more film.* With digital cameras, you don't need to spend money on film or agonize over what type of film will best meet your needs. And if you're careful with your camera's storage, you'll never again find yourself wanting to take that beautiful sunset but powerless to do so because you just used up your last roll of film.
- *Big savings.* No more film means no more processing costs. Think of the amount of money you'll save over the course of a lifetime on

processing alone if you go digital. Although the price of a digital camera might be higher than the price of a comparable 35mm camera, not having to continually pay for film represents a big saving.

· *Instant gratification.* As soon as you shoot a picture, you can immediately check the image. The immediate gratification of digital photography certainly beats the time you used to spend waiting for your film to be developed, or developing it yourself in a darkroom. In addition, being able to check your shots while in the field means you can delete the 'out-takes' as you go along, leaving you with only the best images at the end of the day.

As an added bonus, you're promoting a cleaner environment by using a digital camera, because there are no chemicals, film or canisters that need to be thrown away.

· *Creative control.* Even with all of the benefits described above, one of the main reasons a photographer is likely to purchase a digital camera is for the creative freedom it provides. Buy a digital camera, and your computer acts as your digital darkroom, allowing you to manipulate your images in a variety of ways. For instance, you can eliminate red-eye, change the background of a picture, add or subtract images, turn a black-and-white image into colour and vice versa, crop or rotate your picture and undertake hundreds of other modifications – all at the click of a mouse.

· *It's portable.* A digital camera is small enough to be tucked in your pocket or pocketbook. This means you can carry your camera with you wherever you go and never again miss out on a photo opportunity. That portability also promotes better photography, since the more you shoot, the faster your photography skills are likely to improve.

· *Share the joy.* With your digital camera and e-mail, you can quickly and easily share your photographs with relatives and friends around the globe. And now many websites allow you to set up albums of your images for others to view at their leisure. Just imagine how pleased Mum, Dad and Aunt Isabel will be when you e-mail them the latest snapshots of your bouncing baby.

- *It's good for business.* If you run a small business, a digital camera can be a lifesaver. For instance, estate agents can quickly snap a photo of a property and e-mail it to a client or download it to their website. Photographers and journalists can send images to their editors, whether they're in the next town or halfway around the globe. Antiques dealers who market their goods on auction websites such as eBay can download images and get auctions started on the very same day. For many professionals working in a variety of businesses, a digital camera can become an indispensable tool.
- *Accessible forever.* Although negatives and prints fade and deteriorate when exposed to light, humidity and overhandling, digital images can last forever. With careful treatment, you'll have your digital images indefinitely. And if your printout of an image gets damaged or lost, simply go to the file and print it again. Storing and sharing digital images is much more convenient than having to take negatives to the lab and wait for reprints to be made. It saves you money, too.

The Other Side of the Coin

Even with all the benefits that digital cameras have to offer, there are some drawbacks to digital photography that you should consider before running out and buying your own digital camera. Depending on how you utilize a camera, the level of skill you possess and your dexterity with a computer, digital photography can seem heaven-sent or a complete turnoff.

- *Image quality.* A film or photographic print contains at least ten times as much information as a typical digital camera. To produce a film-like quality photo, a digital camera would need to be filled with so many chips that its price would be astronomical. If you are going to enlarge an image to poster size, you may be better off using a film camera to take the shot. However, if you plan to use the image for a website or your personal online album, a digital camera should work well for you.
- *Expense.* Digital photography requires a financial investment. Although you can find cameras for under £50, the chances are that you will need to spend at least £200, and perhaps a lot more, to get decent-quality images.

In addition to your camera, you'll need a computer, a good colour printer and possibly a larger monitor and a scanner.

· *Darker images.* Digital cameras are not as sensitive to light as film cameras. Out of doors, you probably won't run into any problems. But indoors you may find that it is more difficult to get a decent exposure with a digital camera – and even with a flash, you may need to add more lighting.

· *Poor resolution.* You may find that when you enlarge an image, the resolution suffers and the pixels become visible. (For more on resolution, see 'Image Resolution and Image Quality' in Chapter 2.)

· *Distorted colour.* Sometimes a digital camera gets the colour wrong. It won't be a drastic mistake, such as a red lake or a purple sun, but you might get orange instead of yellow, or purple instead of blue.

In order to save battery power, some digital cameras go into sleep mode automatically when not used for a few minutes. Because of this, you might find that there is a gap of a second or two after you press the shutter before the picture is actually taken.

From SLR to Digital

The American company Silicon Film Technologies has developed an electronic film cartridge called (e)film, which allows 35mm SLR cameras to capture digital images. The electronic film cartridge is an insert that fits into the back of a 35mm SLR body. It uses 64MB of non-volatile flash memory to capture and store up to 24 36-bit 1.3-megapixel digital images, and can be reused thousands of times. With (e)film, you can go digital without the expense of purchasing a new camera – and you can use all of the lenses, flash units and filters you already own. As your requirements change, you can easily switch back and forth between 35mm film and (e)film. And (e)film provides a good option for those wanting to experiment with digital photography before investing in a camera.

Commercial Uses for Digital Photography

Professionals know that digital cameras can provide some benefits that film cameras cannot. Here is just a small sample of how photographers in many fields use digital cameras and digital images to make their jobs easier and improve the work they do:

- Photographers use digital cameras in the studio to shoot everything from fruit to fashions. They can quickly check the resulting image and adjust it as necessary. Once shot, images can be manipulated via image-editing software then e-mailed to clients and vendors.
- Journalists love digital photos because they can be immediately transmitted to their editors via telephone lines or wireless connections. Once in the hands of their editors, the images require no lab processing; they can be used at once. The low resolution of digital cameras is not a problem for newspapers, because they in turn use low-resolution printing.
- Scientists use digital cameras to take videos and photographs through microscopes.
- Security firms are able to utilize the quick processing, easy enhancement and online distribution of digital images.
- Doctors and dentists can use digital cameras for snapping before and after shots of patients. The results can be used for reference, attached to patient charts or submitted with insurance claims.
- Astronomers have used digital image sensors for years. In 1997 NASA's Pathfinder spacecraft carried to Mars a surface rover called Sojourner. Two digital-imaging sensors helped Sojourner negotiate the rough surface of the planet. The orbiting Hubble Space Telescope has a CCD detector with a 1,600x1,600 pixel array.

Is Digital for You?

In the end, it's your decision as to whether or not a digital camera is right for you. Once you've worked out your requirements and considered both the pros and cons of going digital, you'll be able to determine whether a digital camera should be part of your future.

Although no one can predict the future, it seems likely that the trend towards manufacturing cameras with more pixels will continue, with the benefits to the consumer of better resolution and higher-quality photographs. In addition, camera manufacturers are working on improving digital cameras so that the amount of shutter lag is reduced.

CHAPTER 2

Understanding How Cameras Work

Although the cameras of the 21st century are far more sophisticated than previous models, the fundamental principles of taking a photograph have not changed. In order to understand the world of digital photography, you will need to be familiar with some technical terms. By learning the language of digital photography, you will be better able to understand the material in books, magazine articles and websites that cover the topic.

How Digital Cameras Work

All film cameras contain five basic elements:

- *Lens:* A plastic or glass element that collects light and focuses an image on the film.
- *Aperture:* An opening that controls the amount of light entering the camera through the lens.
- *Shutter:* A device that can be opened or closed to control how long the film is exposed to light entering the camera.
- *Body housing:* The plastic or metal outer casing that contains the camera mechanism.
- *Viewfinder:* A lens or frame that lets the photographer view the picture being taken, either directly through the lens (in single-lens-reflex, or SLR, cameras) or through a separate viewfinder (in simple cameras).

Digital cameras are a lot like 35mm film cameras. Both consist of a lens, an aperture, a shutter, body housing and a viewfinder. The big difference between film cameras and digital cameras is the way in which they capture an image. A film camera creates an image when light passes through a lens onto film. The film is coated with light-sensitive chemicals that react when light strikes the film, creating an image. In the developing stage, the image reacts with additional chemicals to produce a printed photograph.

Like a film camera, a digital camera also uses light to create images, but it does so with light-sensitive computer chips (image sensors) rather than film. The chips are categorized as either CCD (charge-coupled device) or CMOS (complementary metal-oxide semiconductor). The majority of digital cameras made today use CCDs, but CMOS chips are gaining popularity quickly. Although they differ somewhat, both types of chips operate in essentially the same way.

CCDs are created using a special manufacturing process that enables them to transport charge across the chip without distortion. CMOS chips are made using the same processes as most microprocessors. Because of differences in manufacturing, there are several differences between CCD and CMOS sensors:

· CCD sensors create high-quality, low-noise images. CMOS tend to be more susceptible to noise (small defects in the image).
· The light sensitivity of a CMOS chip is lower.
· CMOS sensors typically consume little power, while CCDs use a special process that uses lots of power.
· CMOS chips are less expensive to make compared to CCDs.
· CCD sensors tend to have higher-quality pixels and a greater number of them. The data is saved to the camera's memory, which is located on an in-camera chip or a removable memory card or disk. By transferring the images from your camera to your computer, you can access them. Some cameras allow you to transfer images directly to a TV monitor or printer, allowing you to view and print your photos without the need for a computer.

A chip is comprised of rows of tiny light sensors called photosites that capture colour and light, and then convert them into electrical charges. A processor inside your camera analyzes and translates the electrical charges into digital image data. (The brighter the light, the stronger the resulting charges will be.)

Due to these differences, CCDs are commonly used in cameras that create high-quality images with lots of pixels and superior light sensitivity. CMOS sensors tend to have lower quality, lower resolution and lower sensitivity. The other side of the coin is that CMOS cameras cost less and have great battery life. As time goes by, it seems likely that CMOS sensors will improve until they equal CCD devices in most applications.

Colour Your World Digital

Both film and digital cameras create images by reading the amount of light in a scene. A digital camera works much like the human eye to translate that information into the colours that appear in the final image.

Light is made up of three primary colours: red, green and blue. Three receptors in your eye correspond to each of these colours. Each receptor senses the brightness of the light for its particular colour. The brain processes the information to form one multicoloured image.

Like your eyes, a digital camera captures the light intensity – sometimes called brightness value—of the red, green and blue light. It records the brightness value for each colour in separate portions of the image file, or colour channels, then combines them to form a full-colour image.

When images are created using these three primary colours of light, they are called RGB (red, green, blue) images. The RGB system is also called the additive colour system, because when the three colours are combined, or added, in equal quantities, they form the colour white. In our everyday lives, we are looking at RGB images when we view television sets, computer monitors and scanned images.

The source of colour is light. All colours combined form white light. To demonstrate this, place a prism where the light can strike it. The colours separate to form a rainbow spectrum ranging from violet to red. When light strikes a surface, some colours are absorbed while others are reflected. The colours that we see are those that the surface reflects.

Image Resolution and Image Quality

Digital images are made up of pixels. The word pixel is short for 'picture cell' or 'picture element'. Each pixel is a tiny dot, similar to the ones that form the image on a television screen. When a digital image is viewed normally, the pixels blend together (FIGURE 2-1). When the image is magnified on screen, you can differentiate the individual pixels (FIGURE 2-2).

This effect is called pixelization. It is similar to enlarging a traditional print to the point where it develops a grainy look.

FIGURE 2-1: Digital images are made up of pixels – tiny dots similar to those that form the image on a television screen. When a digital image is viewed normally, the pixels blend together.

Photo by Philip Thornberry

FIGURE 2-2: When an image is magnified, you can differentiate individual pixels.

Photo by Philip Thornberry

Each image has a set number of pixels. For instance, low-end digital cameras tend to create images that are 640 pixels wide and 480 pixels tall. To refer to the number of pixels in an image, the term 'pixel dimensions' is used. Sometimes the term 'image size' is also used, although this can be confusing, since image size can also refer to the physical dimensions of an image. (For the purposes of this book, the term 'pixel dimensions' is used to indicate the pixel count, and 'image size' is used when referring to the physical dimensions.)

Resolution is measured in pixels per linear inch, not square inch. For example, a resolution of 75ppi means the image has 75 pixels horizontally and 75 pixels vertically (or 5,625 pixels) for each square inch of image.

The number of pixels per inch (ppi) creates the resolution of an image. The quality of your image will be determined by its resolution. The more pixels per inch, the crisper the image will be. That's why it's important to understand the concept of resolution if you're going to get the results you're seeking from your digital camera.

Images formed from pixels are said to be bitmapped. Each pixel is a shade of grey or colour. The number of bits in an image, or bit depth, indicates how much colour information each pixel can contain. Using 24-bit colour, each pixel can be set to any one of 16 million colours.

Image resolution is also stated in terms of file size. To calculate file size, multiply the total number of pixels by the bit depth of the image, times the number of colours in the image, divided by eight (because there are eight bits to one byte).

You've probably heard the terms 'bits' and 'bytes'. What are people really talking about when they use these terms? Bit stands for 'binary digit' and is the smallest possible unit of digital information. Eight bits equals one byte. Bit depth, or bits per pixel, refers to the number of bits allocated to describing the colour of each pixel. Higher bit depth means a larger file size and more colours. An 8-bit image contains 256 or fewer colours. A 16-bit image contains about 32,000 colours. A 24-bit image contains approximately 16 million colours. A 32-bit image contains literally billions of colours.

Determining the Number
of Pixels You Need

Since higher resolution is a good thing, and the more pixels the better the resolution, you might be thinking that you want to get a camera that can produce images with as many pixels as possible. This is not necessarily the case.

First you must decide how you will use your images; only then will you know how many pixels you need. If you'll be using your images on screen, such as on a website or in an e-mail, a resolution of 72–96ppi is fine, because most monitors are not capable of displaying any more pixels per inch anyway. For onscreen images, you won't need to pay a lot for a digital camera, because most inexpensive digital cameras capture enough pixels to do the job for you.

If you're planning to print your images and you are looking for the best possible output quality, you'll need a resolution of about 300ppi. The number depends on the kind of printer you're using you might need a few more, or you might find that a few less are adequate. The manual that came with your printer should offer the exact resolution guidelines.

If you know the resolution you want your image to be, you can determine the maximum size of the image by dividing the total number of image pixels across (or down) by the desired resolution. For instance, if your camera captures 1,280 pixels across by 960 pixels wide, and your target resolution is 300ppi, simply divide 1,280 by 300 to get the maximum width of the image, which in this case would be 4.25in (110mm). To calculate the maximum height, divide 960 by 300, and you'll find that 3.25in (83mm) is the maximum width. Therefore, your image will be about 4.25 x 3.25in (110 x 83mm) with 300 pixels per inch.

Although you may have surmised that higher resolutions deliver better quality, that is not necessarily true. Printers are adjusted to work with images set to a particular resolution. When you try to print an image file that's at a higher resolution than the printer is set up for, most printers will eliminate the extra pixels, causing the printed image to be of lower quality.

Keeping the Right Size

Every pixel adds to the size of the image file. Large image files not only take up storage space, they also use up lots of computer memory (RAM, or Random Access Memory) when you're editing them. A good rule of thumb is: the file size **x** 3 = the RAM required.

When using image files on a website, the larger the file, the longer time it will take to download it. It's best to keep images at just the 'right' size. In other words, you want the appropriate number of pixels for your output device (screen or printer), but you don't want to exceed that amount. Chapters 19 and 20 look further into using and editing image files.

Adjusting Pixels and Resolution

Your image-editing software will assign a default image resolution to your digital camera image. Typically, this is either 72ppi or 300ppi. To increase or decrease the resolution, you have two choices: resampling or resizing your image.

Resampling

To change the number of pixels per inch, you can use your image-editing software to add or delete pixels, a process called resampling or interpolation. The process of adding pixels is often referred to as upsampling, and the process of deleting pixels downsampling.

At first you may think that upsampling is a good idea. However, problems develop when you add pixels, because the software estimates the colour, saturation and brightness needed to make new pixels. Usually, the results are not as good as hoped for.

If you have an image that contains more pixels than you'd like, it is fine to downsample (delete pixels). But remember that every pixel you delete contains image information, so if you throw away too many pixels you'll be reducing image quality. Make a backup copy of the image in case you are not happy with your results after downsampling; a good rule of thumb is to downsample by 25 per cent or less.

Resizing

A much better approach when changing image resolution is to resize the image while maintaining the original pixel count. For instance, if you have a 4 x 3in (100 x 75mm) image set to a resolution of 150ppi and you double the size of the image to 8 x 6in (200 x 150mm), the resolution decreases to 75. This means your print quality has been reduced. But if you reduce the image size by 50 per cent, to 2 x 1.5in (50 x 38mm), the resolution is doubled, to 300ppi, and you've now actually improved the quality of your print. Chapter 19 looks at ways to resize images using image-editing software.

More About Resolution

The term 'resolution' describes more than image quality. It is also used to describe the capabilities of digital cameras, monitors, scanners and printers. Keep the following in mind.

Manufacturers of digital cameras frequently use the term 'resolution' to describe the number of pixels in the images their cameras produce. For example, a camera's resolution might be stated as 640 x 480 pixels or 1.3 million pixels. These values refer to the total pixels the camera can produce, rather than the number of pixels per inch in the final image. That value is ultimately determined by the photographer when using image-editing software.

To indicate the resolution a camera is capable of recording, the terms VGA (video graphics array) resolution (approximately 640 x 480 pixels), XGA (extended graphics array) resolution (1,024 x 768 pixels) and megapixel resolution (indicating a total pixel count of 1 million or more) are used. Pixel dimensions are a more accurate way of judging the resolution of a camera.

In a similar way, manufacturers of computer monitors use the term 'resolution' to describe the number of pixels the monitor can display. On most monitors you can choose from display settings of 640 x 480 pixels (VGA resolution), 800 x 600 pixels or 1,024 x 768 pixels (XGA). The ppi of your monitor depends on its physical size plus the display setting you choose.

Macintosh monitors are usually set at the factory to display 72ppi. PC monitors are commonly set to display 96ppi. As with digital cameras and monitors, scanner capabilities are also described in terms of resolution. Luckily, scanner resolution is usually spoken of in the same terms as image resolution. A low-end scanner commonly captures a maximum of 300 or 600ppi.

Digital photographs can be created by digital cameras or by scanning an image from a conventional camera and digitizing it.

When printer manufacturers talk about resolution, they're measuring it in dots per inch (dpi). The concept is similar to pixels per inch. Since printed images are made up of dots of colour, the dpi measures how many dots per inch the printer can produce. Typically, the higher the dpi, the smaller the dots, and the better-looking the resulting image will be. You should keep in mind, however, that judging a printer only by its dpi can be misleading. Due to different printing technologies, some 300dpi printers can deliver higher-quality results than some 600dpi printers. There's a closer look at printers and resolution in Chapter 18.

Are dpi and ppi the same thing?
Dpi and ppi are not interchangeable terms. Do not assume you should set your image resolution to match your printer resolution. Printers tend to use multiple printer dots to reproduce one image pixel. Check your computer manual for help when determining the right image resolution for your model.

Overview of Resolution

Opposite is a summary of resolution terms and tips to help you produce high-quality images.

- Image resolution is measured in pixels per inch (ppi). To determine resolution, use this formula: number of pixels across (or down) divided by image width (or height) equals image resolution (ppi).
- For best quality prints, aim for a resolution of 300ppi.
- When using images for onscreen display, 72 x 96ppi is appropriate. However, it's best to think in terms of pixel dimensions rather than image resolution when sizing images for the screen.
- Enlarging a picture can damage the quality of the image. When enlarging an image, either the pixels expand to fill the new image boundaries, or they stay the same size and the image-editing software adds pixels to fill in the gaps. In either case, the image quality deteriorates.
- To increase the resolution of an image, it is best to reduce the image size. Keep the existing number of pixels, and make the image smaller.
- It's best to set your camera to capture a pixel count at or above what you need for your final picture output. You can always delete pixels later if you want a lower-image resolution, but you can't add pixels without risking damaging your image. Another good reason to do this is that although you may want a low-resolution image today for use on a website, in the future you may decide you want to print the image at a larger size – and then those extra pixels will serve you well.
- More pixels will fatten up your image file. You may have enough file storage space to hold big images, but those images will require huge amounts of RAM to edit. And they'll require lots more time to process your edits. On the Internet, a big file means slower downloading of images, and that never makes website visitors very happy. When you send bigger files to your printer, the results are often reduced quality, not better, prints.

CHAPTER 3

What to Look for in a Digital Camera

I t seems as if everyone has jumped on the digital bandwagon, from icons of the photography world to computer and electronics manufacturers. The influx of digital cameras on the market means better models to choose from at lower prices. However, having so many cameras from which to select means you need to do some research before you make your purchase.

Finding a Camera to Meet Your Needs

Although you need to establish a budget before you're ready to go camera shopping, it is also essential that you work out what you want to do with your camera once you've brought it home. Think of shopping for a digital camera as being a bit like shopping for a car. If you're a family of four, you're probably not going to want to get a two-seater sports car. Instead, you're more apt to opt for the people carrier that provides the room for your family to be transported comfortably. But if you're a single man or woman who's looking to make an impression with your vehicle, that flashy sports car might be just the ticket.

How do you want to use your digital images? And what are you likely to take pictures of? If you're planning to use your camera to keep the family up to date on the new baby, then a low-end camera that is simple to operate and takes images that can be used on the Internet may well serve your needs. But if you are a serious photographer, you're likely to be dreaming of owning a digital camera that provides digital images that can rival those you now get from your 35mm camera. If this describes you, then your main concern when choosing a digital camera is resolution. Of course, higher resolution means a higher price, so your budget will have to be big enough to accommodate your desires. If you plan to print your images, you'll probably want to find a camera that provides images of at least 1,280 x 1,024ppi resolution.

Getting the Resolution You Require

Let's see how digital cameras shape up when we compare categories based on resolution and use.

Less than 2 megapixels
· **Pros:** in this category you can find a camera that takes pictures that work well on the Internet (for posting on websites and e-mail); good for the novice who wants an easy-to-use camera
· **Cons:** indoor photos will be of lower quality
· Maximum resolution: 1,024 x 768ppi
· Storage: 4MB

Between 2 and 4 megapixels

· **Pros:** cameras in this category should provide consistent image quality; be good for indoor and outdoor use; and have a good selection of manual controls, including zoom
· **Cons:** More expensive
· Maximum resolution: 1,600 x 1,200ppi
· Storage: 8MB
· Other features: zoom

More than 4 megapixels

· **Pros:** cameras in this category should provide extremely high-quality images; extensive manual controls
· **Cons:** extremely expensive
· Maximum resolution: 2,048 x 1,536ppi
· Storage: 8MB
· Other features: advanced manual controls

Call your local camera and electronics retailers to see whether they hire digital cameras. As digital cameras gain popularity, quite a few outlets are allowing consumers to take advantage of one-day hire. It's the best way to try out a camera before you buy.

Thanks for the Memory

When shopping for a digital camera, you're going to need to take into account the kind of memory the camera uses to store images. Some cameras have built-in (onboard) memory, usually RAM. This means that once the memory is filled up, your picture-taking comes to a halt until you can get to a computer and transfer the images you've just taken to it – a task that can seriously disrupt your photo shoot.

Most new digital cameras are manufactured with removable media for image storage. Simply insert a memory card or disk into a slot on the camera, and you're ready to go.

If you love to travel and want your camera to record the trip, plan to get a camera with removable memory. Removable memory lets you carry extra storage so you'll never be caught unprepared. Two common types are Secure Digital cards and CompactFlash cards.

Cameras without removable media cost less, but it's worth spending the extra cash for two good reasons:

- Once the memory card is filled up, you can simply replace it with another card. There's no need to take a break in your picture-taking.
- With onboard storage, the transfer process to your computer is more time-consuming and less efficient. You have to be able to connect the camera and the computer via a cable, which can be a cumbersome task, and then wait patiently while the images download.

When using a camera with removable media, you won't be pulling your hair out while waiting to get a look at your images. If your camera stores images on a floppy disk, you simply remove the disk from your camera and slip it into the floppy drive on your computer. Then you drag and drop files just like you'd do with any other files on a floppy.

Other types of memory cards work with the assistance of card adapters and readers, which allow your computer to recognize the memory card as a floppy drive. This method of image transfer is much faster and more convenient than using onboard memory.

Some higher-priced cameras feature both built-in RAM and removable memory. Because a camera can access the built-in RAM faster than it can access memory on a removable device, it uses the built-in memory as a buffer. Once you take a picture, the image is saved in the buffer before being sent to the removable memory. This allows you to take the next picture more quickly. And the camera may give you the option of saving your image with various compression modes while the image is still stored in the camera's RAM. (For more information about compression, see Chapter 15.)

The two most popular types of removable media are CompactFlash (up to 256MB Type I and 512MB Type II) and Secure Digital (up to 256MB) cards. Both formats are widely used, so if you choose a camera that uses one of these, you'll be more likely to find replacement cards when you're travelling abroad. And should you decide to buy a new camera, there's a greater chance that your memory cards will work with your next model. (Learn more about removable memory in Chapter 6.)

Long-Term Shooting

If you're planning to spend the day taking photos, whether you're backpacking in the mountains or exploring a tropical island, you'll appreciate the ability of your digital camera to furnish a power supply and enough memory for a full day's shoot. Rechargeable battery packs are now available with many cameras, and if you're travelling or simply planning to spend an entire day pursuing the perfect shot, you'll want to take along a spare battery pack. When your day's shooting is done, simply plug in the charger, and the next day the batteries will be ready to go once again.

Memory capacity is the other key to long-term shooting. If you're on the road, you may find Iomega's PocketZip a godsend. This compact, rechargeable, handheld drive can read both CompactFlash and Secure Digital cards. PocketZip then automatically transfers the images to a 40MB, 50mm (2in) square disk. Once you're back at home, you simply connect the PocketZip drive to your computer's parallel port for downloading to your hard drive.

Memory card capacity, which can take up to 512MB per card at time of writing, means you can take more shots before you have to download. Downloading is quicker too, thanks to USB camera connections (see page 32) and memory card readers that connect to a computer.

Checklist of Secondary Features

Below is a helpful checklist that you can refer to when you're evaluating digital cameras. It is designed to remind you of some of the secondary features of a camera. Remember that the devil is in the details; don't overlook these features or you may make the wrong decision.

- *Batteries:* Find out what kind of batteries the camera uses, and how many shots you can expect to get with a set. Find out if a battery charger and rechargeable batteries are included in the cost of the camera kit.
- *Software:* Does your camera have software for downloading images? Some camera packages also include image-editing software.
- *Computer and printer hookups:* Investigate how the camera connects to your computer. Is it via serial port or a USB (universal serial bus) port? Some models offer wireless transfer, allowing you to send images to a printer or computer using infrared ports, called IrDA (infrared data association) ports.
- *Frame rate:* How long does it take for the camera to clear the image sensor, then store the image in its memory? To successfully take action shots, you are looking for the shortest lag time possible, or a continuous-capture option.

In bright light, LCD screens can be difficult to see. When examining a camera for possible purchase, take it outdoors or to a bright area so you can see how easily the LCD operates in bright light.

What You Can Expect to Spend

Let's take a look at the types of features and benefits of digital cameras available on the market. We'll then review the price points and what you can expect to get for your money.

Inexpensive Cameras (under £30)

Inexpensive digital cameras usually do not have an LCD screen or photo-quality optics. They use lower-priced CMOS sensors, similar to the ones found in webcams. If you're looking for an introductory camera that lets you have fun without providing fantastic image resolution (usually 640 × 480ppi and below), you may want to start with an inexpensive model.

Low-End Cameras (£40–100)

Point-and-shoot digital cameras fall in this category. They are more versatile than the inexpensive models and are fully automatic, so they are easy to use. The disadvantage is you won't get a lot of creative control with a point-and-shoot digital camera. It may or may not have a zoom, but it will usually have an autofocus lens. Most of these cameras use CCD as opposed to CMOS sensors. Resolutions range from 2 to 3 megapixels. Because of their low resolution, printed output is limited to about 100 × 150mm (4 × 6in); nevertheless, these images can be ideal for use on webpages, in e-mail attachments and in newsletters and other documents.

Mid-Range Cameras (about £110–300)

With price tags of under £300, these cameras offer resolutions of usually 4 megapixels plus advanced features such as 3–5X zoom lenses, flash attachments and MPEG (mini-movies) capability. One of the fastest-growing categories of cameras, mid-range multimegapixel cameras are chosen by serious photographers who are seeking creative control of their camera's settings and the ability to generate prints up to approximately 200–255mm (8 × 10in) and 280 × 355mm (11 × 14in).

High-End/'Prosumer' Models (about £400–700)

If your camera budget is in the £400–700 range, you may want to consider a high-end ('prosumer' or semipro) digital camera, which offers extensive controls and expensive optics such as stabilized long zooms. Typically, cameras in this category use CCDs that are 4–6 (and sometimes even 8) megapixels and have very precise optics and two or three different metering systems. Some high-end models offer TTL (through-the-lens) viewfinders and compatibility with more than one type of recording media (such as CompactFlash and Secure Digital), plus compatibility with external flash units or their own dedicated units. These cameras provide high-quality images of between 4 and 8MB.

If you are seeking a camera that allows you to print images up to 305 x 430mm (12 x 17in), you'll find that a 'prosumer' or semipro digital camera can provide those sizes with good detail.

Professional Cameras (£850 and above)

If money is not an object, you may want to consider the professional digital cameras adapted from 35mm and APS (Advanced Photo System) SLR cameras. These cameras often utilize three different image sensors – one for each colour – so they capture great colour and provide superior resolution. Their image sensors tend to be 6 million pixels, and a few models have even more. The great advantage of these cameras is that most of the features and accessories designed for their film counterparts also work with the digital versions.

Cameras for Special Needs

There are all sorts of digital cameras out there, but some are designed to meet specific needs.

Desktop video cameras can capture still images, but these will be low resolution and not suitable for much but casual Internet use. Because the camera is attached to the computer, desktop digital video cameras are extremely limited in their uses.

Webcams

Designed for video conferencing and Internet telephony (using the Internet to make phone calls), the video camera captures your image and sends it out via the Internet.

Handheld Digital Video Cameras

Handheld digital video cameras allow you to wander far and wide in search of the ultimate picture. Some of the models are extremely sophisticated, such as the digital camcorder, the Canon Optura Pi, which allows you to record images in three different modes: normal movie mode; digital photo mode (to which you can add narration or sound effects); and digital motor drive mode, which permits you to take 30 frames per second. When you're watching your kid's football game, this camcorder will help you record the action. The Canon Optura Pi allows you to take two hours of digital movies or 700 digital photos on one mini DV (digital video) cassette. Capture images on a floppy disk, view them on your TV or download to a DV-compatible computer.

Handheld Computer Cameras

The useful and popular digital camera is being incorporated into more and more devices, ranging from laptop computers to PDAs (personal digital assistants).

For instance, the Handspring company has developed a full VGA digital camera, called eyemodule2, that allows the Handspring Visor handheld computer to take snapshots. The eyemodule2 snaps into the Visor handheld via its Springboard expansion slot to enable the user to capture and view images in black and white or colour in a variety of different formats. Handspring users can take pictures with the eyemodule2 in full VGA to download and print high-resolution pictures, take Handspring Visor screen-sized snapshots saved in a compact format to conserve memory on the handheld, or record mini video clips.

If you own a Palm handheld organizer, you may want to investigate a camera such as the Kodak PalmPix. This works in a similar fashion to a desktop camera – attach it to your organizer, then shoot, store and review 24-bit colour VGA pictures. Maximum resolution is 640 × 480ppi, so your images are going to be low-resolution, and each image takes up about 100K of Palm memory.

CHAPTER 4

Buying the Digital Camera That's Right for You

N ow that you've learned about pixels, resolution and memory and have read all about what your money can buy, let's walk through the steps you'll need to take to get a digital camera that's just right for your purposes.

A Step-by-Step Guide

Step 1: Establish your budget. How much can you realistically spend on your new camera? After all, the best camera in the world won't do you any good if you simply cannot afford to make it your own.

Step 2: Decide if you want to print photo-quality pictures. And if you do, what size do you want them to be?

Step 3: Know what kinds of pictures you're planning to take, then find a camera with the features that enable you to shoot them. Asking yourself the following questions can help you determine just what features you'll need.

· Are you a casual photographer, a serious amateur or a professional? The answer to this question will determine how many manual controls your camera should have.
· Will you be photographing action shots, such as your children's games? Or are you planning to take primarily stationary photos? The answers to these questions will determine the best viewfinder and lens for your camera. You may also want to look for a continuous shooting mode and consider how many shots it can take in a row.
· Will you be shooting indoors? This will determine the quality of the flash you need.
· Will you be taking wide-angle shots of landscapes? Close-ups such as flowers in the wild? Telephoto scenes such as portraits? Your answers will help you decide the focal length of the lens you need, and whether or not you should buy a zoom lens, auxiliary lenses or macro mode. (For more on lenses see Chapter 7.)
· Will you be travelling or spending a lot of time out on location? If so, you'll want to consider the memory and power supply capabilities of the camera.

Step 4: Begin looking at various models of digital cameras. Start with the Internet and photo magazines, and make comparisons as you go. Once you've narrowed your search to three or four models, you're ready to get your hands on the real thing.

You want to make sure that you like the way the camera feels when you're holding it and shooting with it. If you are left-handed, you will be especially concerned about how the camera feels in your hand.

Step 5: Look for a well-designed camera. Go to a reputable retailer so you can test out the cameras you're considering. Does the camera feel well-balanced? Inspect the camera controls to be certain you can utilize them effortlessly – you don't want to miss a great shot because you couldn't quickly prepare the camera to take it.

Step 6: Get ready to put down your money. Where do you want to go to make the purchase? You may decide that your local retailer is the best place to buy your camera, or perhaps you've found an incredible deal on a website such as eBay. Remember to consider the postage charges, check closely for any hidden extras, and don't be fobbed off with something else if the model you want is currently out of stock.

Watch out for 'unbundling', a practice by unscrupulous retailers of removing items such as lens caps, battery chargers, memory cards and software that are usually included in basic camera packages, and selling them separately for an additional charge.

Investigating the Choices

There are many places to turn for information about the digital cameras currently available in the marketplace. The quickest way to begin is by getting onto the Internet. There you will find all kinds of websites that contain information about digital cameras in general and specific makes and models. There are also sites that offer comparison shopping so you can compare various models. Start by searching on 'digital camera'. You'll be amazed at the number of websites your search will uncover.

If you have a particular manufacturer in mind, you should check out their website. But make sure you also explore impartial digital photography sites, many of which compare features of various models, giving the pros and cons of each.

Researching Cameras on the World Wide Web

Check the following websites to get product information, compare prices and read reviews:

Buy a Camera
www.buyacamera.co.uk
DealTime
www.dealtime.co.uk
Digital Camera Resource
www.dcresource.com
DigitalCameras
www.digitalcameras.com
I Want One of Those
www.iwantoneofthose.com

Kelkoo
www.kelkoo.co.uk
MoreCameras
www.morecameras.co.uk
7DayShop
www.7dayshop.com
Which? Online
www.which.co.uk

The Internet also offers an avenue for communicating with other digital photographers. Many photography websites feature message boards where you can chat with others who share your interest in digital photography. You also might want to log onto newsgroups, sites where people ask and answer questions on many topics, for discussion of various models of digital cameras. Or look into photography clubs, both online and offline, for opportunities to discuss digital cameras with kindred spirits.

The Latest News on the Digital World

Jump on the Internet to explore what's happening in the digital world or connect with others who share your interest in photography. There are numerous resources you can use, and you'll probably enjoy surfing the Internet to see what's out there.

To point you in the right direction, below are listed a number of websites that offer up-to-the-minute trends, news and reviews about digital photography, general photography and related subjects.

Apogee Photo
www.apogeephoto.com
BJP Online
www.bjphoto.co.uk
Black and White World
www.photogs.com/bwworld
Blind Spot
www.blindspot.com
Cheese Magazine
www.cheesemagazine.com
Digital Photo Imaging
www.digitalphoto.com
ePhotozine
www.ephotozine.com
Focus Online
www.focalfix.com
Kodak eMagazine
www.kodak.com
OnLinePhotography
www.onlinephotography.com

Outdoor Photographer
www.outdoorphotographer.com
PC Photo
www.pcphotomag.com
Photobetty
www.photobetty.com
Photo District News
www.pdnonline.com
Photo Insider
www.photoinsider.com
Photomag
www.photomag.co.uk
Photo.net
www.photo.net
Photoserve
www.photoserve.com
Shutterbug Online
www.shutterbug.net
ZoneZero
www.zonezero.com

Words and Pictures

The next best thing to being out in the world photographing people and places is reading about it. To find print publications on photography, start with your local newsagent or library. On the following page are some photography magazines that cover both digital and general photography.

- *British Journal of Photography*
- *Digital Camera*
- *Digital Camera Buyer*
- *Digital Photo*
- *Digital Photography*
- *PC Photo*
- *Photomag*
- *PhotoTechniques*
- *Photography Monthly*
- *Popular Photography*
- *Shutterbug*

There are a number of very good general photography and digital photography magazines, both print and online, that you can use in your search for information about digital cameras. These are wonderful resources for discovering the very latest news and trends in the world of digital photography.

Going, Going, Gone – Buying at Online Auctions

If you're in the market for a digital camera, you might consider browsing in cyberspace. One source for cameras of all types – and many other items – is an online auction. There are several, with eBay probably being the most widely known. Here are several auction sites you may want to take a look at:

Amazon Auctions
www.auctions.amazon.com
eBay
www.ebay.com
Egghead
www.egghead.com

uBid
www.ubid.com
Yahoo! Auctions
www.auctions.yahoo.com

Auction sites offer both used and new merchandise from retailers and private sellers. Here are a few tips to help make your online buying experience a satisfying one:

- Don't be afraid to ask questions. If you look at the pictures of the item and still have doubts, don't hesitate to e-mail the seller and get your questions resolved.

- Investigate the seller's record. In most cases, you can view feedback from other people who have dealt with the seller. If the feedback is negative or nonexistent, you should think twice about buying from this seller.
- Talk to others. If you examine the seller's feedback and you have a doubt or a question, contact the last few bidders who have purchased from this seller and ask them how they fared in their dealings with him. If they say that all went well, you are unlikely to have a problem.
- Make sure you know the current market value of the item you're considering. Check other websites to see what the going price is for the camera in which you are interested.
- Pay with a credit card. This way, if a problem does arise, you can put the transaction on hold or cancel it.
- Some online auctions offer a service that lets you review the item you're buying before payment is released to the seller.
- Insure the package. Make sure the insurance covers the replacement value of the item.

Don't get carried away with auction fever. Just as in a live auction, buying at an online auction can cause bidding wars. Don't fall victim to one and pay too much for your camera.

Find out the return policy of the retailer, so that if a problem with your camera should arise you'll know that the retailer will correct it to your satisfaction, without charging you a fee.

Is It Time to Buy?

Buying a digital camera is a lot like buying a computer: it's hard to know if you should buy one now or wait for a while. Should you pick from the models that are currently on store shelves or wait for technology – which is constantly evolving – to come out with a model that has even more bells and whistles, and probably carries a lower price tag as well?

In 1965, Gordon Moore, who was then research and development director for Fairchild Semiconductor and who later went on to become one of the founders of Intel Corporation, predicted that the density of transistors on a silicon chip would double every 18 months. As the ability to put more and more transistors on a chip increases, the cost per unit of computing power declines. Today, Moore's Law, as his prediction came to be called, has turned out to be extremely accurate – in the past three decades or so, the number of transistors on a standard silicon chip has grown from 2,300 to 28 million.

The same expansion of technology applies in the digital world, meaning that if you wait about six months, you'll be able to buy an even better camera for less money. And if you plan to keep up with the rapidly changing digital world of photography, you can count on replacing your camera system every two to three years.

The first hurdle is to decide whether to purchase a digital camera at all. Once you've decided you do want to take the plunge into the world of digital photography, it becomes a question of when to make the leap. But the truth is that new and better models will always be on the horizon. Meanwhile, while you're agonizing over whether to buy a digital camera, you could be out there enjoying one.

What do I ask?
How much does the camera cost? What resolution does it have? How much storage does it provide? What format does it use for storage? How does it transfer photos to my computer? Does it have optical or digital zoom? Does it use resolution interpolation? Does it offer voice or video recording?

Looking After a Digital Camera

Once you bring home your digital camera, you will want to protect your investment by taking good care of it.

The first thing to do is to purchase a sturdy camera bag. Make sure it's roomy enough to hold all your supplies, including your batteries and camera accessories. Most manufacturers of camera bags now make them to fit digital cameras. Although digital camera bags are smaller in size, they offer the same high-quality materials as 35mm camera bags. When storing your camera, use your camera bag to protect it from bumps, dust, heat and humidity. Remove the batteries before storing it. Never put your camera near strong magnetic fields, such as those found in electric motors – if you do, your image data may sustain damage.

Put together a cleaning kit and keep it either in or near the bag so you can clean off the inevitable finger smudges, dust and grit that will settle on your camera and accessories. This kit can be simply a package of lens tissues, or you may want to invest in some microfibre cloths, a lens brush and cleaning solution.

 Whatever you do, don't attempt to use paper tissues or paper towels to clean your camera lenses – even in an emergency or when there's nothing else to hand – as they can seriously scratch your equipment. Always use specially made lens tissues or microfibre cloths.

When shooting in a wet or dusty place, put your camera inside a plastic sandwich bag in which you've cut a small hole for the camera lens. Use a rubber band to seal the opening. The bag will keep moisture and grime out of your camera.

Although your digital camera can tolerate slightly more heat than 35mm cameras, you should still protect it from high temperatures. Never leave your camera in a hot car – one parked in the sun will turn into an oven, and you may come back to find your camera 'baked' beyond repair. At the beach, a plastic bag will protect the camera from sand and salty air, and covering it with a light-coloured cloth will reflect sunlight. Once indoors, never place your camera near radiators or other heat sources. If your camera is exposed to direct sunlight and has become hot, let it cool down again before using it.

Cold can also cripple your camera. When shooting outside in cold temperatures, place your camera underneath your coat to protect it from the elements. Remember that batteries will weaken in the cold, so you may want to take extras along with you.

When bringing your camera inside after it has been exposed to the cold, protect it from condensation by wrapping it in a plastic bag or towel until it reaches room temperature. If condensation does occur, do not take the camera back out into the cold, or the moisture can freeze up its operation. Take out the batteries and the memory cards, and leave the camera open until everything has dried out.

Treat your camera with a little TLC and it will provide you with enjoyment for years to come.

CHAPTER 5

Image Sensors

D igital cameras use image sensors to capture pictures. As you already know, there are two types of image sensors: CCD (charge-coupled device) and CMOS (complementary metal-oxide semi-conductor). Not long ago, the only image sensors used in cameras were CCDs. Both types capture light in essentially the same manner, but they differ in the ways they are manufactured and how they process images. CCDs are created using a special manufacturing process that enables them to transport charge across the chip without distortion. CMOS chips are made using the same processes as microprocessors.

CCD Versus CMOS

Because of differences in manufacturing, there are several differences between CCD and CMOS sensors. But what do these technical differences mean to you in practical terms?

- CMOS tend to be more susceptible to noise (small defects in the image). CCD sensors create high-quality, low-noise images.
- CMOS chips are less expensive to make than CCDs.
- CCD sensors tend to have high-quality pixels and more of them.

What is noise?
Noise comes from the light sensors in your digital camera, resulting in an image that appears grainy, similar to a snowy image on your TV screen. Noise tends to appear when you choose an ISO rating that is too high, or when you use image-editing software to correct an underexposed area.

Due to these differences, CCDs are commonly used in cameras that create high-quality images with lots of pixels and superior light sensitivity. However, CCD chips have a problem with blooming, which means that they tend to produce undesired halos around very bright highlights.

Blooming can occur when there is an area of concentrated light in your frame. It can happen in very bright daylight or studio light, or if there is a bright source of glare in your scene. For instance, if you're shooting a picture of the relatives gathered at the Christmas dinner table, the glowing candles on the table can cause blooming. The camera's CCD sensors will overload, then the charge from the overexposed pixels seeps into adjacent cells, causing a coloured halo to form around bright or shiny objects, or as random flashes of light.

Early CMOS sensors tended to have lower quality, lower resolution and lower sensitivity. Now, however, technology is advancing to such a degree that CMOS image sensors are likely to continue to improve until they equal CCD devices in most applications. Canon have already gone down this route, starting with their EOS D30, aimed at professional users.

Prevent blooming by using a neutral density filter when shooting in full sunlight or when shooting a well-lit scene with a darker foreground.

CMOS cameras currently offer several advantages, including lower price tags and great battery life. In addition, CMOS chips are better at capturing highlights than CCDs, making them a better choice for shooting objects such as jewellery or capturing the glint of sunlight on the ocean.

The Super CCD, developed by Fuji, uses a different pixel arrangement from other CCD sensors; its SR chip has two photodiodes at each site. Nikon uses a system called JFET LBCAST in its digital SLR cameras.

Digital Technology Is Out of This World

NASA, the National Aeronautics and Space Administration, in a quest for lightweight imaging systems for interplanetary spacecraft and other applications, undertook research to develop a computer chip that would be more advanced than the CCDs already developed.

In 1992, the NASA Jet Propulsion Laboratory (JPL) expanded the CCD technology to create complementary metal-oxide semiconductor active pixel sensors (CMOS APS). Today, the CMOS technology that enables consumers to snap digital photos also allows spacecraft to gather images for use by NASA.

Once such craft is NASA's NEAR (Near Earth Asteroid Rendezvous) Shoemaker, which orbited 433 Eros, a near-Earth asteroid 19 million miles from Earth, for a year, providing scientists with an abundance of data that included more than 100,000 close-up images. In 2001, the NEAR Shoemaker became the first spacecraft to touch down and operate on the surface of an asteroid, generating even more detailed images of the asteroid's surface for scientists to study.

Image Sensor Resolution

In the previous chapter it was explained that digital photographs are made up of tiny squares called pixels. When you take a photo with a digital camera, each of these pixels is captured by a single photosite on the image sensor. A computer and printer then use the pixels to display or print photographs.

To create the image, the computer divides the screen or printed area into a grid of pixels. Then it uses the values stored in the digital photograph to specify the brightness and colour of each pixel in the grid. This process is called bitmapping, and the resulting digital images are called bitmaps.

Once a digital image is printed or displayed on a screen, its quality is determined in part by the number of pixels used in creating the image (its resolution). The number of photosites on the image sensor determines the maximum number you are able to capture.

It's important to understand how image sensors operate in order to grasp the concept of resolution. You will need to understand resolution in order to understand the workings of a digital camera, scanner and printer. This knowledge will help you choose, buy and operate the equipment required by a digital photographer.

Aspect Ratio

The aspect ratio is the ratio of image width to image height, and it varies among image sensors. The ratio of a square is 1:1 (the width equals the height), and the ratio of 35mm film is 1.5:1 (it is 1.5 times wider than it is high).

The aspect ratio determines the shape and proportions of your digital images. When an image has an aspect ratio that differs from the device on which it is being displayed or printed, the image must be cropped or resized to fit. It's a bit like trying to fit a square image on a rectangular piece of paper.

The aspect ratio of a camera can be calculated by dividing the larger number in its resolution by the smaller number. For instance, if a sensor has a resolution of 1,536 × 1,024, you would divide 1,536 by 1,024 for an aspect ratio of 1.5.

Understanding aspect ratios can be of help when you're evaluating a digital camera before purchasing and when you are manipulating images with software programs.

Colour Depth

Although resolution is an important determinant of the quality of an image, another equally important factor is colour depth. This is the term used to refer to the number of colours in an image, which is also called pixel depth or bit depth. Older computers have displays that only show 16 or 256 colours. Most new computer systems display what is known as 24-bit true colour. The term true colour is used because the systems display 16 million colours, which is about the same number as can be discerned by the human eye.

There is more about colour (bit) depth in Chapter 17.

Frame Rate

Digital cameras experience two delays that affect the photographer's ability to capture fast-action shots. The first delay, just a second or two, occurs once you have pressed the shutter button and before the camera actually captures the image. This delay is known as the refresh rate. During this small delay, the camera is preparing to take the picture by clearing the image sensor, setting the white balance to correct the colour, setting the exposure and focusing the image. Finally, if needed, the camera fires the flash and then takes the picture.

The second delay, called recycle time, is a lapse that lasts from a few seconds up to half a minute and happens when the captured image is processed and stored.

How quickly a series of photos can be taken in succession is known as the frame rate, shot-to-shot rate or click-to-click rate. Both of the delays described above affect the frame rate. If the frame rate is not quick enough, the photographer can miss a shot.

Some cameras offer a burst mode, which lets the photographer take photo after photo while holding down the shutter button. To increase the frame rate, these cameras often decrease the resolution used to capture the images. Some digital cameras reduce recycle time by temporarily storing a series of images in the camera's RAM until they can be processed. A camera with burst mode enables the photographer to easily capture action shots. Another way of beating refresh and recycle times is to lock onto your subject by pressing the shutter halfway down and then keeping it there. This will preset the focus and exposure on whatever you're pointing the camera at, so that when you're ready to shoot the camera will fire almost instantly. More information on burst mode and action shots is found in Chapters 10 and 12.

Sensitivity

If you've purchased film for an analogue camera, you will have encountered the ISO (International Standardization Organization) number, which appears on the film package. This number, such as 100, 200 and 400, represents the speed, or sensitivity, of the film. The higher the number, the more sensitive the film is to light. ISO numbers indicate that the film speeds are doubling as the numbers increase.

Image sensors are also rated using ISO numbers, which are meant to be approximately equivalent to film ISOs. The lower the ISO of an image sensor, the more light is needed for a good exposure. A camera with a higher ISO will enhance freezing motion and shooting in low light. Image sensors' ISOs can range from 100 to 1,600, but most consumer digital cameras are rated at ISO 100–400. This is the reason that digital cameras often do not work well in low-light conditions, and why many come with built-in flash. Information on operating a flash and taking photos in various lighting conditions can be found in Chapters 8 and 13.

There are some digital cameras that allow you to change the sensitivity of the image sensor, such as the Olympus C-3030 and S-2500 and the Nikon 950 and 990. You probably won't be able to boost the ISO beyond 400, but at least this will allow you to shoot in most interiors.

Remember that when you boost the ISO, you're more likely to encounter noise problems with your images.

Image Quality

The resolution of an image affects the size of the image file to some degree. The higher the resolution, the greater the number of pixels that must be stored, resulting in a larger image file.

In order to make image files more manageable, most digital cameras store images in a format known as JPEG, which was developed by the Joint Photographic Experts Group. The JPEG format compresses the images; the photographer specifies to what degree they are compressed.

Compressing files compromises image quality, so having some control over compression is useful. You can choose to store fewer images of higher resolution, resulting in better prints. Or you can increase compression and store more images of low resolution, suitable for sending via e-mail or posting on a website but not of a good enough standard for high-quality prints. Compression is discussed in more detail in Chapter 15.

CHAPTER 6

Image Storage (Memory)

With film cameras, the film serves two purposes: it records the image, and it stores the image. With digital cameras, two separate devices perform these functions. The image sensor records the image, and a storage device stores it.

Removable Memory Versus Fixed Storage

The recent development of new storage media and associated readers allows you greater freedom than in the early days of digital photography. More expansive memory capabilities mean more pictures per load, giving greater convenience and the ability to capture more high-resolution images on a storage device. When you're equipped with the latest storage media in the field, you'll have the satisfaction of shooting for long periods without interruption.

Thanks to advances in technology, new storage media appear to be introduced every several months, but not all with the same degree of acceptance or success. At the time of publication, the following main types of removable media were available for digital photographers:

· CompactFlash (general use)
· Secure Digital (general use)
· xD-Picture Card (Fuji and Olympus)
· Memory Stick (Sony and some others)
· SmartMedia (used with a decreasing number of digital cameras).

All forms of removable media allow the photographer to remove the storage device when it is full and replace it with another.

Several factors affect the number of images that you can store in your digital camera:

· The resolution of the images
· The amount of compression used
· The capacity of the storage media.

When calculating how much storage capacity you'll need in a camera, you should consider the number of shots you normally take with a film camera. (For instance, if you typically use two rolls of film with 24 shots each, that's 48 shots.) Your camera's memory will need to accommodate the same number of shots, calculated by multiplying the number of images the storage device holds by the number of storage devices you are willing to carry with you.

Flash Memory Cards

Older models of digital cameras are likely to use floppy disks or PC cards. Almost all newer models use a form of flash memory.

Flash memory cards use SRAM (static RAM technology that holds data without electric current). They come in many sizes, shapes and storage capacities. They do not require batteries, and they do not lose images when the power is switched off. Flash memory cards take up little space and use up little power.

Their small size and light weight make flash memory cards convenient and easy to carry, so you can take lots of them with you and replace them as necessary during a photo shoot.

Types of Flash Cards

There are a number of different types of flash cards. In the past, the cards were not interchangeable. Today, however, card readers have been developed to help bridge the gap between various models of camera and memory cards. (There is more on readers later in this chapter.)

Since flash memory devices have no moving parts, the cards are almost indestructible. *Digital Imaging* magazine online recounted the story of Ron Rosenberg, a radio commentator from California, USA, whose water plane crashed while he was attempting a landing, sending his HP 200LX handheld computer to the bottom of a lake. Several months later, a diver found the computer and returned it to Rosenberg. Inside he found his SanDisk CompactFlash (CF) card containing 3,000 phone numbers. Carefully drying off the CF card, he inserted it into a computer, and it worked perfectly. Such is the durability of today's flash memory cards.

PC Cards

Flash memory cards first began gaining wide acceptance when PCMCIA (Personal Computer Memory Card International Association) cards were introduced several years ago. Today, they're frequently referred to as PC cards. These small cards, about the size of a typical business card, were originally designed to be utilized with laptop computers.

Most of the PC cards adhered to ATA (AT Attachment) standards. ATA was designed as a standard interface for storage devices such as disk drives and flash memory cards for the mobile computer market. An ATA-compatible card was guaranteed to work with any system supporting ATA, including digital cameras. An ATA-compatible card should also work with all major operating systems, including DOS, Windows and Mac OS.

Unfortunately, not all ATA-compliant flash cards work with all digital cameras. Most major vendors do support ATA, but some camera manufacturers do not. To determine whether your digital camera supports ATA, check the operating manual.

Initially, PC cards were offered in three types: Types I, II and III. The three types were identical in length and width but differed in thickness. Type I was 3.3mm thick, Type II was 5mm thick, and Type III was 10.5mm thick. Today, Type II is the leading format for PC card storage devices. Type II cards are currently available in several storage capabilities, from 128MB to the 4GB card expected soon. However, few consumer or compact cameras use Type II PC cards, which have mainly been used for upmarket professional cameras.

CompactFlash and Secure Digital Cards

The majority of consumer SLR cameras today use CompactFlash cards for memory storage. CompactFlash uses the same memory storage devices as PC cards, but does so in a much smaller package, measuring 45 x 35mm. CF cards are available in two types: Type I, which is 3.3mm thick; and Type II, which is 5.0mm thick.

Not long ago, Delkin Devices increased the capacity of its CompactFlash (Type I) memory cards from 128 MB to 512MB and its CompactFlash Type II cards to 4GB. Part of their eFilm lineup, these cards are designed to store the maximum number of high-resolution images taken with today's larger megapixel digital cameras.

Lexar Media has developed its USB-enabled Pro Series CompactFlash cards, also with 4GB of data storage. The faster write speeds (over ten times that of a standard card) make these cards ideal for use with top-of-the-range digital cameras.

Secure Digital is a major competitor of CompactFlash and is used by a large number of camera manufacturers, primarily Panasonic. Like CompactFlash, Secure Digital is based on ATA technology. In comparison with CompactFlash, Secure Digital cards are a similar size and are less expensive, and have grown in popularity to the point that they are now able to also be fitted into a wide range of other devices, including TVs and DVD players and PDAs.

Memory Card Adapters

Memory card adapters allow CompactFlash, Secure Digital and other cards to be read as if they were standard PC cards. After putting the memory card in the adapter, you insert the adapter into your computer's PC card slot or into a PC card reader. The PC card appears as a drive on the computer desktop. You then simply drag and drop image files from the PC card to the hard drive.

Memory Card Readers

Various manufacturers have developed memory readers, which also allow you a means of quickly and easily transferring digital images from digital cameras, as well as from MP3 players, PDAs and the Internet. The readers enable you to copy and move digital files stored on the memory cards from one digital appliance to another, or between computers, external storage drives and the Internet.

One such reader is the Vector Flash Memory Reader from SmartDisk. Another is ActionTec's PC805 PC Card Reader, which accepts three types of media without adapters: Type I and II AT Flash PC; CompactFlash; and

Secure Digital cards. The external reader connects to the parallel port and keyboard connectors of PCs.

Another popular card reader is the eFilm Pocket Reader from Delkin. It's tiny (about the size of a keyring ornament) and lightweight, and requires no cables so it's ideal for use by digital photographers in the field. A USB connector built into the back of the unit allows it to plug into any USB port on a laptop or desktop computer. Three versions are available for CompactFlash, Secure Digital and IBM Microdrive.

Disk Adapters

Disk adapters allow your floppy disk drive to read memory cards. The card is inserted into the adapter, and then the adapter is put into the floppy drive. Next, you drag and drop image files from the floppy drive to your hard drive, as you would with any other file from a floppy disk. These adapters are, however, being superseded by memory card readers.

Storage on the Go

Not long ago, Minds@Work introduced a portable storage device called Digital Wallet. The Wallet offers 3, 10 or 20GB of portable storage in a compact, handheld unit. The storage media from your camera is inserted into the Wallet, and in a few seconds your images are downloaded. The Wallet works with most media types, including CompactFlash, Secure Digital and IBM Microdrive. Once you're back at your computer, you simply download your images from the Wallet.

New Digital Camera and Storage Media

In 2001 Sanyo announced a new type of digital disk camera. The IDC-1000Z iDshot digital camera was the first camera to utilize the iD PHOTO disk. The iD PHOTO media standards were developed jointly by Sanyo, Olympus Optical Co. and Hitachi Maxell.

Sanyo's iD PHOTO magneto-optical disk features 730MB of storage and is capable of saving both still and moving images. It holds approximately two hours of moving image recording at 160 normal mode (160 x 120 pixels), or about 11,000 still images. The camera achieves high-definition still images at 1.5 megapixels and moving image clips at 30 frames per second with high-quality VGA images.

DataPlay's optical technology holds 500MB of data on digital media about the size of a 20p piece. Extremely inexpensive, the DataPlay digital media offer a low-cost alternative to flash memory cards. Digital cameras from Toshiba accommodate the DataPlay digital media.

New products are being developed and marketed all the time, and the instances here are examples of devices that have been successful on the market. Check the websites and magazines listed in Chapter 4 to keep up with the range of new and exciting digital products.

Before inserting a memory card into your digital camera, it may need to be formatted to receive your digital images. Check your camera's operating manual for more details.

Caring for Your Memory Cards

The memory cards you buy for your digital camera represent a considerable financial investment. Not only that, they act as your camera's 'film', allowing you to do what you like to do best – taking pictures. You'll want to get the most that you can from your memory cards and protect the images you've taken once they are stored there. Follow the suggestions below to ensure that your cards work well:

· Wait for your camera to finish recording the data on the card before trying to take the card out of your camera. Never remove the card while the camera is still processing information.
· Don't switch off the power to the camera while it is accessing the card.
· There are certain areas of the memory card that you should avoid touching with your fingers. On the CompactFlash card, avoid the connector on the bottom of the card. With Secure Digital, don't touch the gold section at the top of the card.
· Protect your memory cards from heat, humidity, dirt and static electricity. If your card gets dirty, use a soft cloth to gently wipe it off.

CHAPTER 7

Lenses

A primary component of digital cameras is the lens, which is made of optical glass or plastic that has been designed to gather light reflected from the subject and project it onto the image sensor in the digital camera. The lens serves as the eye of your camera, determining what your camera can see and how well what is seen is conveyed to the camera's image sensor. No matter how many megapixels a camera has, if it has a low-quality lens, the picture quality will be inferior. That's why it is important to know the details of the lens on any camera you are considering purchasing.

Focal Length

One of the most important characteristics of a lens is its focal length. On film cameras, the focal length is the measurement of the distance between the centre of the lens and the film. On a digital camera, the focal length measures the distance between the lens and the image sensor. In both cases, focal length is measured in millimetres.

On a 35mm camera, a lens with a focal length of less than 35mm is known as a short, or wide-angle, lens. One with over 65mm is considered a long, or telephoto, lens. Lenses with focal lengths between 35 and 65mm are considered normal. The 50mm lens is the most common, or standard, lens.

With digital cameras, the actual focal lengths do not provide useful information. For this reason, manufacturers typically provide the equivalent 35mm focal lengths.

By changing focal lengths, you immediately change the lens's angle of view and its magnifying power. The term angle of view describes how much of a scene the lens captures. A short lens has a wide angle of view, meaning that it can capture a wide expanse of a scene. A long lens has a narrower angle of view so it can isolate small sections of the scene.

Magnification goes hand in hand with angle of view. A short lens, with its wide angle of view, requires all the objects in a scene to be reduced in size in order to fit into the image sensor. It has the effect of pushing the subject away from you. Conversely, the long lens, with its corresponding narrow angle of view, will have the effect of pulling objects in a scene close to you, causing them to appear larger.

When you choose a lens for your digital camera, the first question to ask yourself is how you plan to use your camera. If you want to photograph landscapes, buildings and interiors, wide-angle lenses will best suit your needs. If you are interested in shooting portraits or nature scenes, telephoto lenses will do the trick. A middle ground would be a normal lens.

Determining Focal Length

How is focal length determined to be wide, normal or long? When the focal length of a lens is close to the diagonal measurement of the film format, the lens is called normal, or close to the magnification of the human eye. When the focal length is longer than the film diagonal, it's known as long or telephoto. When the focal length is shorter than the film diagonal, it is referred to as short or wide-angle.

Categorizing lenses is based on the film size being used, so a given focal length might be considered normal on one type of camera, wide-angle on another and telephoto on a third. The chart below lists some common film formats and the focal lengths of their normal lenses.

Film format	Film diagonal (mm)	Normal lens
35mm	43mm	50mm
2¹/₄ x 2¹/₄in	90mm	80mm
4 x 5in	163mm	150mm

The same parameters determine the wide-angle, normal and telephoto lenses of digital cameras as film cameras.

To make it simpler for photographers to understand, references to digital camera's lens focal lengths are often referred to with the corresponding equivalent in 35mm camera lens. For instance, the spec sheet for the PowerShot S300 Digital Elph camera describes the lens as being 5.4–16.2mm with a 35mm film equivalent of 35–105mm.

Keep your lens free of dust and grit and you will protect the glare-reducing coating and the glass itself. A lens cleaning kit that includes a blower brush and lint-free tissue is a must. Protect your lens by keeping a UV filter on it at all times.

Maximum Aperture

When taking a picture, you press the shutter release and the shutter opens to emit light from the scene to be focused onto the image sensor. To get the ideal exposure, just the right amount of light must strike the image sensor. If there is too much or too little light, you'll need to adjust the amount of light. One way to do so is by opening or closing the lens's aperture, an adjustable opening that regulates how much light passes through the lens. 'Stopping down' the aperture makes it smaller so that it lets in less light. Opening it up lets in more light.

The size of the aperture is measured in f-stops, which control the depth of field. With few exceptions, each f-stop lets in half as much light as the next larger opening and twice as much light as the next smaller one. From the largest opening to smallest, standard f-stops are as follows: f/1, f/1.4, f/2, f/2.8, f/4, f/5.6, f/8, f/11, f/16, f/22, f/32 and f/45. This can be a little confusing because the larger the f-stop, the smaller the amount of light that is let into the camera. The easiest way to think of f-stops is in terms of fractions: just as $\frac{1}{16}$ is less than $\frac{1}{8}$, an f-stop of f/16 is smaller than, and lets in less light than, f/8.

You won't find the full range of settings on any one lens. In most cases, the standard lens on a digital camera is in the f/2–f/16 range.

The maximum aperture of a lens determines by how much it can be opened. The maximum aperture is also referred to as the maximum iris, or the speed of a lens. Although lenses are referred to by their focal length, the description of a lens also carries a second number, such as 2.0 or 3.5, which indicates the maximum aperture of the lens. Larger maximum apertures, such as f/1.8, let in more light than smaller apertures, such as f/3.2, allowing you to take better shots in low-light situations.

Focusing Methods

Although most digital cameras with non-interchangeable lenses are either fixed focus or autofocus, there are other possibilities.

Fixed Focus

A fixed-focus lens is a simple lens with no moving parts; the lens cannot be adjusted. The camera captures sharp images of any subject within a certain distance from the lens, usually from 2m (6ft) to infinity. Objects outside that range will appear out of focus. In general, objects that are too close to the camera will appear blurred because the focus is adjusted for a specific distance from the camera to infinity.

The minimum focusing distance specifies how close to the subject you can place the camera. That is, it controls your ability to take close-up shots. If you are planning to take a lot of close-up shots, be sure to check the minimum focusing distance of any camera you are thinking of purchasing.

For many years most simple cameras, such as the many versions of the Kodak Brownie, had fixed-focus lenses. Millions of people took pictures and were happy with their snapshots, and since the pictures were seldom enlarged, they provided acceptable quality.

Today, low-end digital cameras typically are equipped with fixed-focus lenses. If you're a first-time digital photographer, you may want to start with a camera that has a fixed-focus lens. However, you should note that fixed-focus lenses provide the photographer with fewer options and, therefore, fewer creative possibilities.

Manual Focus

Manual focus permits the user to adjust the focal point from three different distances, which allows for more creative control. Typically, the settings are macro mode (extreme close-ups), portrait mode (for subjects about 4m/12ft from the camera) and landscape mode.

Autofocus

An autofocus camera offers a more precise and versatile system than a fixed-focus camera. Cameras with autofocus automatically adjust the focus depending on the distance of the subject from the camera. Sometimes an autofocus camera will also offer focus lock. This feature lets the photographer stipulate exactly what object the camera should focus on. Usually this is accomplished by centring the subject in the viewfinder, pressing down the shutter button halfway to 'lock' the focus, then reframing your shot and taking the picture.

Some top-end digital cameras allow the photographer to set the focus point a specific distance away, such as 30cm (1ft) or 1.2m (4ft). When taking a shot of a scene with many elements, this can be a useful feature. For instance, if you are shooting a picture of a woman standing in front of a statue, the autofocus may lock on the statue rather than on the person.

Although autofocus adds to the expense of a camera, in the majority of cases it renders better images. With the demand for print quality in digital images on the rise, more and more manufacturers are producing digital cameras with autofocus.

Types of Lenses

Lenses are generally categorized as integrated, interchangeable, zoom and macro.

Integrated Lenses

An integrated lens is part of the camera and is not detachable. Some integrated lenses allow you to add supplementary lenses. Typically, supplementary lenses screw onto the lens barrel thread or slip over it using a friction mount. A supplementary lens changes the viewing angle of the lens or allows it to focus more closely than it would in macro mode.

Interchangeable Lenses

An interchangeable lens can be detached from the camera and replaced with another lens that has the same type of mount. Professional photographers rely on interchangeable lenses to create desired effects, depending on the situation they are shooting. If you are considering purchasing a digital camera with an interchangeable lens, make sure you investigate the number and types of lenses that can be used.

Zoom Lenses

A zoom lens has a variable focal length, meaning that it allows you to adjust the focal length over a variety of ranges. The range of focal lengths a zoom lens covers usually is specified by its magnification. For instance, a 3x zoom lens will enlarge or reduce the subject in an image by three times. In general, the equivalent range when used on a 35mm camera also is given, such as 38–114mm.

Zoom lenses are either optical or digital. An optical zoom lens truly changes the amount of the subject falling on the image sensor. This results in every pixel in the image containing unique data, providing a final photo that is crisp and clear. The advantage of an optical zoom is its ability to take more detailed pictures of faraway objects. An optical zoom's magnification level is measured in degrees, such as 2x or 3x. A 2x optical zoom means that if the camera's minimum focal length is 50mm, the lens has the ability to take photos up to 100mm.

The term optical zoom refers to a lens that magnifies an image using a real multifocal lens, as opposed to a digital zoom, which only enlarges the centre by 50 per cent.

A digital zoom takes a part of the normal image and enlarges it to give the appearance that you have zoomed in on the subject. The digital zoom adds new pixels to the image using interpolation.

If you are given a choice, you should always choose optical zoom over digital zoom. The digital zoom lens is not really zooming. By enlarging part of the image, it is only giving the appearance of having zoomed in on the subject. With an optical zoom, you can vary the focal length. When you zoom in, the focal length increases (SEE FIGURE 7-1 OVERLEAF), and when you zoom out, the focal length decreases.

FIGURE 7-1:
Using a zoom
lens, the photog-
rapher was able
to capture
exquisite detail
on an old piano.

Photo by Philip Thornberry

Macro Lenses

A macro lens allows you to focus while standing very close to your subject in order to take close-up shots. It is designed to maintain superior sharpness and contrast when focused on a subject that is very near the camera. Most macro lenses are made in a single focal length. Although some have wide-angle or telephoto focal lengths, most macro lenses have a normal field of view.

A lens can be made of glass or plastic elements. Glass tends to provide higher optical quality and greater resistance to scratches. Lenses are coated to cut down on reflections that can occur on the surfaces of lens elements, causing blurring of the image. Read reviews of lenses in photography magazines and on websites to determine which ones are of highest quality.

Some digital cameras can focus as close as a couple of centimetres from the subject. This capability will be appreciated by the nature photographer hoping to catch the opening buds of wild orchids in the spring or tiny crabs scampering down a beach. A macro lens can even come in handy around your own home – with a macro lens on your digital camera, getting down on your knees for a close-up shot of a new kitten or puppy can provide delightful results.

In addition to shooting close to the subject, the macro mode allows you to use your camera like a scanner to make digital images of illustrations, prints of photographs and other objects that would otherwise be scanned on a flatbed scanner.

Taking a Closer Look at Macro Photography

The world is a marvellous place, especially when viewed close up. Digital cameras that have non-interchangeable lenses typically feature a macro, or close-up, mode. To get the best effects from your macro photography, keep these tips in mind:

- Check your camera's manual to see what the range is for your macro mode. (It can vary from a few centimetres to as much as 460mm/1ft 6in.) Then stay within that range.
- It's difficult to know how your image will really look if you depend solely on your viewfinder. You're better off previewing your shot with the LCD screen. This is true of all digital photography, but especially when shooting in macro mode.
- If your camera is equipped with a zoom lens, set it at the maximum wide-angle position. Otherwise, it will be difficult to focus correctly to get that macro shot.
- If your camera has an adjustable ISO setting, set the sensitivity higher. This increases the depth of field, bringing your macro shot into focus.
- Forget about using your built-in flash, as this has usually been designed to work further than the macro range.
- It's essential to keep the camera steady, so use a tripod.
- If your camera offers a manual focusing feature, use it to take great close-up shots.

- All digital cameras offer autofocus. Sometimes an autofocus camera also will offer focus lock. This feature lets you stipulate exactly what object the camera should focus on, usually by centring the subject in the viewfinder, pressing down the shutter button halfway to 'lock' the focus, then reframing your shot and taking the picture. Review the playback to make sure the focus was correct.

Lens Accessories

One drawback to less expensive digital cameras is their lack of interchangeable lenses. However, if a camera has a screw-thread ring inside the front of the lens barrel, it can probably accommodate supplementary lenses and filters. When shopping for a digital camera, you may want to look for one with an interchangeable lens capability, especially if you plan to take many different types of photos.

Filters

Photographic filters are used to correct the colour of light or provide a special effect. Some important filters are as follows:

- *UV (ultraviolet):* a UV filter removes ultraviolet light, which commonly shows up in the background of distant shots as a blueish haze. The UV filter causes your photo to look more like the scene you see when taking the picture. However, a UV filter is also a great tool for protecting your camera lens, so you may want to leave it in place even when you are not photographing landscapes.
- *Polarizing:* polarizing filters remove glare caused by reflected light and tend to improve colour saturation. A polarizing filter will darken a blue sky and add richness to colours.
- *Light:* balancing filters are available in either neutral density or colour temperature converters. When taking pictures in brightly lit situations, a neutral density (grey) filter will reduce the light coming through the lens so that you can use a wider aperture to get less depth of field. Colour temperature converters change the colour of light to balance the type of film being used. But in a digital camera, colour temperature

converters are unnecessary since you can achieve the same effect by using your camera's colour (white) balance.

Lens Hoods

A lens hood, or lens shade, hinders unwanted light from striking the lens. It also affords your lens some protection from knocks and bumps.

Lens Caps

A lens cover is a little thing, but it can offer big protection for your camera's lens. Lenses on digital cameras are particularly susceptible to scratching and smearing, as the cameras are so small that your fingers may end up on top of the lens.

Look for a camera with a lens cap that automatically covers the lens when the camera's power is turned off. Barring that, attach your lens cap to the camera with a string to help prevent your losing it. Try to hold onto the lens cap that came with your digital camera; because the lens caps are so small, it's hard to find replacements. If you do come across a lens cap that fits your digital camera, it might be a good idea to invest in a spare.

Evaluating a Lens

When purchasing a digital camera, many people forget to consider a very important component of the camera: the lens. Along with the image sensor, the lens is the part of the camera that will most critically affect the quality of your photographs. The tips below will help you judge the lens on the camera you're considering purchasing:

· Who made the lens? If it is a manufacturer known for making high-quality optics, such as Nikon, Canon or Olympus, this is an indication that your images will be crisp and colourful.
· Does the lens use plastic or glass optics? Generally, glass optics are better, although high-quality images can be made from both.
· Can you attach filters to the lens?

· Test-drive a zoom lens. Stand 3–4m (10–12ft) away from a group of people, look through the lens and zoom all the way out to wide-angle. How many people are in the shot? Try out the telephoto end the same way. Remember to consider the types of shots you'll be taking. The aim is to get as much original image data into the camera as possible.

· Is the zoom lens motor-driven? Or can you zoom manually? If it's motor-driven, you'll use up your batteries faster. You also will want to note how long it takes to zoom.

If the 2x or 3x zoom lens on your camera doesn't provide enough power for you, you may want to take a look at the Canon PowerShot Pro90 IS. Its 10x zoom offers a range of coverage equal to a 37–370mm lens on a 35mm camera. Telephoto lenses are perfect for capturing shots of distant subjects, but they make it difficult to hold the camera steady enough to get a crisp picture. Canon has designed its image stabilizer so the PowerShot Pro90 can get clear photos, even at full zoom.

CHAPTER 8
Flash

Unless you're a professional photographer, the chances are that the camera you're using – whether film or digital – has a built-in flash. When shooting indoors, such a flash will work adequately if the subject you're shooting is within 3–4m (10–12ft). Although your built-in flash will permit you to take a photo in a low-light environment, it will not provide the same effect as natural lighting. Rather, pictures taken with an on-camera flash tend to look similar, since the flash produces a flat light that minimizes surface textures.

Limitations

You will need to experiment a bit to see what your camera's flash can and cannot do. Most built-in flash units are small and are designed to light up subjects close by. If you're in a situation where you're shooting a large area, such as at a sporting arena, the flash can't possibly illuminate the whole scene. If you try to shoot the entire stadium, you'll probably end up with an underexposed photo.

Some more expensive models have stronger flashes that work at longer distances. Or they may have a hot shoe, a mounting device that enables the addition of a flash unit.

Try out your flash in several different situations. Take a series of indoor shots with your subject standing or sitting at different distances from your camera. Take shots of your subject in front of a light source, such as a window, with and without the flash to see how a flash can 'fill' in darkened areas.

Settings

Some digital cameras allow you to adjust your flash unit to one of the following modes:

Auto Flash

Here, the camera gauges the available light and fires the flash if needed. In certain situations, the resulting image can be well lit, but the background may be almost black. Some top-end cameras avoid the problem of silhouettes by firing the flash if they detect a backlit situation.

Because every flash has a useful range, the effects of the auto flash will depend on how bright a light it produces and how far the light has to travel. Flash light becomes dimmer the further it has to travel. The further away the subject is from the camera, the less light will be reflected back to the camera. Objects closer to the camera will appear lighter than objects in the background.

When you are taking a photo of a scene with multiple subjects at different distances from the camera, the exposure cannot be correct for all of the subjects. In most cases, those closest to the camera will be properly exposed. The further the subjects are from the camera, the darker they will appear in the picture.

Fill Flash

The fill flash mode allows you to add light to an image without affecting the exposure settings. A photographer will turn on the fill flash mode when he or she wants to add light to the backlit (shadowed) areas in the scene being photographed. For instance, if a subject is standing in front of a large window, turning on the fill flash will help illuminate the subject's face so that he or she does not look like a dark shadow. A photographer can also use fill flash in normal sunlight when he or she wants to fill in the shadows on the subject.

Fill flash is a great feature of modern cameras, both digital and analogue, because it shortens editing time by avoiding the problem of unwanted shadows in the first place.

Night Flash

Night flash, or night portrait mode, combines a flash exposure with a longer capture speed. This mode is ideal for shooting room lights or an evening sky with a brightly lit subject. If your camera does not have night flash, the next best thing is to use fill flash, although the results will not be quite as good. Another option is to take separate pictures of the foreground and the background, and blend them using editing software.

Red-Eye Reduction

This mode helps to reduce the 'red-eye' effect that occurs when a flash is reflected in the subject's eyes. Red-eye reduction works by firing a low-power flash, or burst of flashes, just before the primary flash is fired. The low light causes the iris of the eye to close slightly, diminishing the chance of the flash being reflected there.

The bad news is that red-eye reduction is not always totally successful. The good news is that if your subject does end up with red eyes, you can correct the problem with image-editing software because you're using a digital system.

There are five ways to combat red-eye in pictures:

· Move the external flash further away from the camera lens.
· Tell the subject not to look directly at the camera.
· Increase the overall lighting in the area where the picture is being taken.
· Use the red-eye reduction mode on your camera.
· Use image-editing software to remove red-eye.

Slow-Sync Flash

Some cameras offer a slow-sync flash, which increases the exposure time beyond the normal flash. This mode helps illuminate background shadows that normal flash mode misses. The slow-synchronized mode works by allowing the shutter to remain open longer than normal so that the background appears lighter.

Sometimes when using slow sync, fast-moving objects or a shaky camera can cause images to blur. To avoid blurring in your photo, use a tripod and/or photograph stationary objects. Alternatively, you can always use blur creatively for interesting effects. For instance, using slow sync to photograph moving cars can create blurred trails in the resulting image, conveying a sense of speed in the photo.

External Flash

This mode lets you use a separate flash unit similar to ones that are used with 35mm SLR cameras. In this mode, the camera's built-in flash is turned off and you must manually set the correct exposure to work with the flash.

If your digital camera's built-in flash is leaving you with underexposed images, there are a number of flash enhancement systems available, which can be used with any digital camera or film camera with a built-in flash, hot shoe or PC synchro contact.

Additional Light Sources

Hot spots and red-eye are two of the problems that can arise when shooting with a flash. If your camera works with an auxiliary flash unit, you can move the flash away from your subject, which will help reduce these problems. However, if your digital camera does not accept an auxiliary flash, your best bet may be to turn off the flash and use another source of light.

Slave Unit

Your digital camera may be designed with a built-in flash and no connection for an additional flash unit. However, you can still get the benefits of an external flash by using a device known as a slave unit.

Many digital cameras discharge an invisible pre-flash before the actual flash. The problem with standard slave units is that this pre-flash triggers them, so they fire prematurely. Using a slave unit that has trigger mode two is the answer to this problem.

A slave unit is a small battery-operated flash unit with built-in photo-eyes. The slave unit fires a flash when it senses another flash of light. There are some slave units that are designed specifically for use with a digital camera. If you're taking photos at a wedding reception and the room is dimly lit, you can sprinkle slave units throughout the space. Then, when you take a picture, all the slave units will go off at the same time, allowing you to get a great shot in the now well-lit room.

Additional Lights

If you already own studio lights for use with your film equipment, they will come in handy with your digital camera. If not, you might decide to purchase some inexpensive photoflood lights, the same type that are used with video camcorders.

Another option is to use what you already have at home. Look around the house for creative solutions. Placing a subject near a window may provide enough light to do the trick. Turn on small table lamps, or purchase clip-on lights at a DIY or hardware store for extra lighting. Or make a backdrop using a white sheet or board, and you've created your own mini photography studio.

Whatever your light source, do not aim it directly at your subject. You'll get far better results if you allow the light to bounce off background and onto your subject. This technique is called bounce lighting.

Getting the Correct Exposure

Controlling the amount of light that hits the CCD in your digital camera is one of the necessary components of capturing an image successfully – and it is one of your biggest challenges as a digital photographer. Too much or too little spoils your final image, with the result of rendering it too light or too dark. Having certain tips and tools at your disposal, along with lots of practice, will allow you to wrestle with the unpredictability of light and come up a winner.

Photographers use grey cards, available from camera shops, to help get correct exposures. Place the grey card in front of the subject so that it is in the same light as the subject. Move in close to the card so that all you see in the viewfinder is the grey card. Tip the card so that it appears as bright as possible and has a slight glare. Then tip it again to eliminate the glare and read the camera meter to find the proper settings.

Film Speed

Conventional film cameras use film of different speeds, or ISO ratings. In a similar way, CCDs in digital cameras have ISO ratings that indicate their sensitivity to light. The higher the ISO rating, the less light is needed for full exposure. For instance, a CCD with an ISO rating of 400 needs less light to achieve full exposure than a CCD with an ISO rating of 100.

If your camera allows you to change the sensitivity of the CCD from one shot to the next, you can adjust the ISO setting as the lighting dictates. For instance, in a low-light situation you can increase the ISO setting to get as much light as possible striking the CCD.

Backlighting

When you are photographing a subject with a bright area behind that is casting the person in shadow, you're encountering the challenge of backlighting. Most people know that when shooting outside on a sunny day, the sun should always be behind the photographer. But sometimes it is simply not possible for you to set up a shot this way.

The sun creates backlighting when it is behind your subject, casting shadows on him or her. However, you should be on the lookout for other backlighting situations caused by things such as white walls or windows so you can take action to avoid an underexposed photo.

A problem arises when backlighting occurs because the camera's light meter reads the scene as being too bright and shuts down the aperture to compensate. The end result is a photograph that is underexposed.

What's the solution? First, if your camera has an exposure override, you can easily correct the problem by opening up the aperture or slowing down the shutter. By giving your subject a few more stops of light, your image will come out looking good.

You cannot always avoid backlighting, but there are ways to take a great photo anyway, even if you can't move the sun or other source of light. Overleaf are some tips to keep in mind.

- Start with the rule we all learned with our first cameras: position your subject so that the sun is behind you, not him or her.
- Let the subject stand where he or she is, but move yourself so that the sun is behind you.
- Turn on your flash. Your camera may refer to this mode as fill flash mode, as it allows you to use your flash in any light condition.

Shooting at Night

Taking photographs at night is easier today thanks to digital cameras and a few good accessories. Because you can preview your shot using the LCD screen on your digital camera, you can be quite certain of what your exposure should be. When shooting at night, be sure to use a tripod, to hold the camera steady, and a cable release or self-timer. Experiment with different shutter speeds.

CHAPTER 9

Batteries, LCD Screens and Viewfinders

Digital cameras are powered by batteries. The LCD and the flash tend to drain battery power. Using the wrong batteries or shooting without conserving your batteries may result in your running out of battery power quickly. Familiarize yourself with the different types of batteries, LCD screens and viewfinders.

Alkaline Batteries

Alkaline batteries work in most digital cameras. Although you may be tempted to buy these economical batteries, they are not a good choice as they won't last very long. In cold weather, alkaline batteries will die very quickly. Only turn to alkaline batteries if you're caught short and there's nothing else available. Alkaline batteries are primary batteries, meaning that they're not rechargeable. For a digital camera, your best bet is to use rechargeable batteries and a battery charger.

Choosing Rechargeable Batteries

When selecting your digital camera, be aware of what batteries it uses. A rechargeable, or secondary, battery is usually designed to have a lifetime of between 100 and 1,000 charge cycles, depending on the materials from which it is made. Rechargeable batteries used in digital cameras generally last from 500 to 800 charge cycles, or about one to three years of average use.

NiMH

Nickel metal hydride (NiMH) batteries are the most popular batteries for digital camera use because they are rechargeable, nontoxic and relatively inexpensive. Since they're designed to be used with power-draining equipment, they can offer you more pictures per charge than other types of batteries. According to one manufacturer, NiMH batteries can last 40 per cent longer than the same size NiCad (nickel cadmium) battery. In digital cameras, NiMH batteries can typically run three to four times as long as an alkaline battery from a single charge.

NiMH batteries need to be run through three to six charge cycles before they reach maximum power. Keep this in mind if you are using your new camera in a situation where you need to get the maximum number of shots out of each recharge.

NiMH batteries are also popular because they don't have problems with memory effect. Made from nontoxic materials, NiMH batteries are more environmentally friendly than other types of batteries. The battery retailers we checked with when writing this book all recommended NiMH batteries for use in digital cameras.

NiCad Batteries

NiCad (nickel cadmium) batteries are the most widely used type of rechargeable household battery, used in small portable devices such as cameras, radios, laptop computers and mobile phones. You can recharge them quickly, and they last for hundreds of charge cycles. NiCad batteries perform well in low temperatures, but they do have a problem with memory effect. Cadmium is an expensive, and toxic, metal. Consequently, producing NiCad batteries is expensive, as is disposing of them. To combat the increased costs, some manufacturers are actively recycling components of NiCad batteries.

Never mix batteries of different types in the same camera. For instance, don't mix NiMH batteries with NiCad batteries.

Rechargeable batteries, especially NiCad batteries, run into problems if they are not fully drained before being recharged. Attempting to recharge a battery that hasn't fully lost its charge can result in its not taking a full charge, or not delivering its full capacity, or both. When you recharge a NiCad battery that is half full, it will always need to be recharged when half full and will only take half a charge. The memory problem is caused by potassium-hydroxide crystals building up inside the battery cells. The build-up interferes with the chemical process of generating electrons during the next battery-use charge. To solve the problem, either leave the camera and LCD on to fully discharge the batteries or utilize a battery charger.

Li-Ion

Li-Ion (lithium-ion) batteries are one of the newer types of rechargeable batteries. They last about twice as long as NiMH batteries, they don't lose their charge as quickly when stored, and they don't have memory-effect problems. However, they are harder to find (you can't pop to the corner shop for one) and cost more than other types of rechargeable batteries.

Battery Chargers

When buying your camera, find out if it comes with a battery charger. The newest battery chargers rely on microprocessor technology to provide rapid charge to your batteries in about one to three hours. (Otherwise, it can take up to 12 hours to recharge batteries.) Another advantage of a battery charger with microprocessor control is that it can determine when a battery is fully charged. Then it will either trickle charge or shut off completely. This prevents overcharging of batteries.

When purchasing a battery charger, find out if it can trickle charge the batteries. Once the batteries have been fully charged, trickle chargers continue to supply a small charge to them. There are differing opinions on the effectiveness of trickle charging, and some battery manufacturers do not recommend it. The best battery chargers send only an occasional pulse charge, rather than a continuous low rate of charge, to a battery that is already charged. Excessive trickle charging tends to dry out the electrolyte that makes a battery work, thereby ruining the battery.

Here are some things to consider when choosing a battery charger:

· Can it charge either NiMH and NiCad batteries?
· How long does it take to charge a set of batteries?
· Can it condition NiCad batteries?
· How many cells can it charge at one time?
· Does it have an optional 12V power cable so you can plug it into your car's cigarette lighter when you're on the road?

Every battery has two ratings: volts and amp-hours (Ah). The Ah rating also may be shown in milliamp-hours (mAh), which are one-thousandth of an amp-hour. For instance, 1 Ah is equivalent to 1,000 mAh.

Getting the Most From Your Batteries

The batteries you purchase for your digital camera reflect a financial investment. Maybe even more important to a photographer, they must be operating properly or a photo shoot will come to a standstill. To get the most from your batteries, follow these pointers:

- Keep batteries clean. A clean battery will make a better connection with the camera.
- Use a cotton bud and lighter fluid to get rid of dirt.
- Do not leave a battery in a charger for more than 24 hours. This will shorten the life of the battery.
- New batteries need to be broken in. Fully charge then discharge them several times so that they attain their maximum capacity.
- Use the battery on a regular basis. In general, a battery needs to be used once in two to three weeks.

Keeping Batteries Ready to Use

When charging and using batteries, you should always do so in sets so that you know all the batteries in one set are totally drained. Either label or colour-code them to help you keep track of their use. To avoid problems, do not mix and match old and new batteries, and always have at least one spare set of batteries.

Getting ready to take off on a photo shoot? Be sure to check your batteries first. Always keep an extra set charged and ready to go. If you're planning on a long day of taking pictures, it might be a good idea to take several sets of batteries with you. That way, you should be prepared for almost all eventualities.

When your batteries wear out, don't throw them away; instead, recycle them to help protect the Earth. In some cases, they can be returned to the shop where you purchased them. Many shops gather old batteries together and then recycle them.

Prolonging Battery Life

You may have heard it said that batteries will keep their charge longer if you store them in the freezer, especially if you're planning on storing them for a long time period. The current thought on this subject seems to argue against the point. The battery retailers we spoke with did not recommend storing batteries in the freezer for two reasons:

1. Freezing can cause liquid electrolyte to freeze and stress, or perhaps rupture, the seals.
2. Most batteries are designed to work between –38°C (–40°F) and 37.5° C (100°F), so putting batteries in a freezer will have no impact on their life span.

Extremely high temperatures can have a negative effect on battery life, so you'll want to avoid storing batteries in direct sunlight, but there is no need to put them in the deep freeze. Simply store your batteries in a cool, dry place and make sure to recharge them fully before using them again, and you should reap the most from them.

Avoid problems with charging due to dirty contacts on the battery or charger. Periodically clean the contacts with a cotton bud dipped in methylated spirits or lighter fuel.

When using your camera, be aware of how long it runs on each charge. When you start to notice that a charge isn't lasting as long as it used to, it is time to think about replacing your batteries. No matter how well you care for them, batteries do not last forever.

Buying Batteries on the Web

To keep your camera going, you're going to need to keep your supply of batteries well stocked. You may find it easier to track down the batteries you need for your digital camera, particularly lithium-ion ones, by looking on the Internet. Here are a few popular sites that offer batteries for sale online:

A Battery Pack
www.abatterypack.com
Allbatteries
www.allbatteries.com
Amazon.co.uk
www.amazon.co.uk
Battery Direct
www.batterydirect.com
Internet Cameras Direct
www.internetcamerasdirect.co.uk

Lawtronics
www.lawtronics.co.uk
Lithium Battery Co.
www.lithiumbattery.co.uk
More Battery Store
www.more-battery.com
Stuff UK
www.stuff-uk.net
The Register
www.theregister.co.uk

LCD Screens

FIGURE 9-1:
One great advantage of a digital camera is the LCD screen, which allows the photographer to preview a shot.

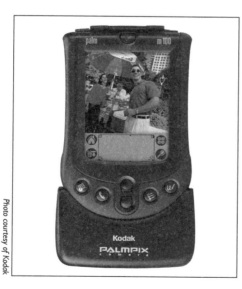

Photo courtesy of Kodak

Most digital cameras utilize an LCD screen (SEE FIGURE 9-1), which is a small monitor that displays an image before you take a photo or once it is shot and stored in the camera. The LCD also displays menus that allow the photographer to change the camera settings and delete images from memory.

An LCD will eat up battery power. Turn it off and use the optical viewfinder. When you do use the LCD display, reduce the brightness, or use the black-and-white mode if your camera has one.

An LCD screen's size is specified in inches. As with a TV set, the screen is measured diagonally and is between 2 and 3in (50 and 75mm), although some cameras have larger ones. LCDs offer several useful purposes:

· The photographer can use the LCD screen to preview the picture before he or she snaps it.
· Once the image is taken, the photographer can review it on the LCD screen and decide to keep it or delete it.
· The LCD screen lets you scroll through your saved images. Depending on the screen on your digital camera, you may see just one image or thumbnails of a group of images.
· The LCD screen often provides you with a true TTL view of the scene being photographed.

If your camera has both a traditional viewfinder and an LCD, you can frame pictures using either one. However, when shooting close-ups, most cameras will force you to use the LCD to avoid parallax error. (See the next section, 'Viewfinders', for more information.)

Some cameras with LCDs do not have traditional viewfinders. This requires the photographer to compose shots using the LCD. It can be difficult to shoot pictures using the LCD for framing, because you need to hold the camera a little way away in order to see what you're shooting.

There are other downsides to LCD monitors, including the following:

· They add extra weight to the camera.
· They eat up battery power.
· Shooting in bright light can make it difficult to see the LCD.
· An LCD can add to a camera's price. In some camera packages an LCD is an optional accessory, while other manufacturers include it in the basic camera outfit.

It's difficult to see some LCD screens in bright sunlight. To solve that problem, you may want to purchase a hood for your LCD screen. One source on the Internet is Hoodman Corporation *(www.hoodmanusa.com)*, which offers four different sizes of hoods that are designed to work with more than 30 brands of digital cameras and digital camcorders.

Viewfinders

Good digital cameras offer both LCD screens and optical viewfinders. Optical viewfinders provide a view of the scene you are shooting, but they don't show you whether or not it is in focus. In addition, the view they show is not exactly the same view as seen by the lens. For the most part, this is not a problem, although it can produce difficulties in close-up photography, when parallax causes the view you see to be slightly different from the one the lens sees.

If your camera has a metering system, there may be intelligence (lights and dials) shown in the viewfinder. There may also be markings to indicate what your camera sees when in telephoto or wide-angle mode. Some cameras provide an indicator in the viewfinder that lets you know when the strobe is recharged.

As with popular 35mm SLRs, some digital cameras come with viewfinders that provide TTL viewing so that what you see is what you get. Light entering the lens is divided by a prism so that part of the light displays the image in the viewfinder, and the rest passes directly through the image sensor.

Some optical viewfinders offer a dioptre adjustment for photographers who normally wear glasses. The photographer can change the setting so that he or she can see though the viewfinder without wearing glasses.

What Is Parallax Error?

On many film and digital cameras, the viewfinder utilizes a separate window from the camera lens. The viewfinder is located about 25mm (1in) above or to one side of the lens, so it 'sees' the subject from a somewhat different angle than the lens. The image, however, is captured from the point of view of the lens, not the viewfinder.

The viewfinder contains black lines, called framing marks, that help you set up your shot to avoid cutting off the top of the picture, an example of parallax error. As you get closer to your subject, the greater the chance that parallax error will occur. Some cameras utilize framing marks on their viewfinders to indicate the framing boundaries for close-up shots. Your camera manual can explain the uses and meanings of the framing marks featured on your camera.

Why have both an LCD and a viewfinder?
The advantages of having both an LCD and a viewfinder, put simply, are these: the LCD allows you to review and delete images on the camera, and the viewfinder ensures easy picture-taking, especially on sunny days when using an LCD can be troublesome.

When checking an optical viewfinder, consider the following:

- Can you easily see through the viewfinder?
- Is it a size you can use without trouble?
- If you wear glasses, can you comfortably see through the viewfinder while wearing them?
- Is there any information in the viewfinder?

If your camera features an LCD screen, think about these points:

- Can you see it well?
- Does it work well in bright light?
- How about in dimly lit situations?
- Is it big enough to be easily used?

CHAPTER 10

Creative Controls and Other Features

Let's admit it: sometimes we're taken in by eye appeal. That sleek, high-tech digital camera... well, it's hard to resist. Pick up the camera and check how it feels in your hand. Still, regardless of how appealing it may be aesthetically, you want to use your digital camera to produce amazing pictures. In this chapter, we examine some of the creative controls that digital cameras offer.

Creative Controls

Your digital camera comes with a number of creative controls. These automatic features may include the following:

· Autoexposure
· Autoflash
· Autofocus
· Colour balance.

In most situations you'll want to use these automatic systems. After all, even professionals frequently take advantage of them. But there will be times when you seek greater creative control. In those instances you will need to override the automatic settings. Let's take a closer look at what these automatic settings can do, what effects can be accomplished by overriding automatic controls, and how you go about doing so.

Autoexposure

As noted in Chapter 5, controlling the amount of light that hits the CCD in your digital camera is one of the necessary components of capturing an image successfully – and it's one of the biggest challenges faced by any digital photographer. Too much or too little light will spoil a final image, causing it to be too light or too dark.

Although it's very convenient to let the camera automatically adjust the exposure, there are times when the camera can be fooled and it's best to take the matter into your own hands. Of course, it's possible to use an image-editing software program to correct any 'mistakes' of exposure. But image information in the shadowed or highlighted areas will have been lost and cannot be reclaimed.

The odds of creating a properly exposed photo are greater when you manipulate the exposure while shooting, rather than trying to correct mistakes while editing.

There are a number of circumstances when you might choose to control exposure yourself. For instance, if you are shooting into the sun, photographing on a snowy mountainside or shooting a brook in a shady forest, you will probably not let the camera automatically set the exposure, since these are situations that can fool the camera.

To control the amount of light that exposes the image, the photographer can adjust either the aperture or the shutter speed. When using automatic exposure control, the camera is set to make one or both of these adjustments.

Some mid-range and top-end cameras give the photographer more creative control over f-stops and shutter speeds. Low-end digital cameras are typically fully automatic. These are the exposure systems that you are most likely to encounter:

- *Fully automatic:* the camera automatically selects both the aperture and shutter speed.
- *Aperture priority:* you choose the aperture (controlling depth of field), and the camera sets the best matching shutter speed for desirable exposure results.
- *Shutter priority:* you choose the shutter speed (controlling motion), and the camera selects the best matching aperture for best results.

In a brightly lit scene, such as on a snowy mountainside, the camera will use a fast shutter speed and a small aperture. In a low-light situation, such as a shady forest, the camera uses a long shutter speed and a wide aperture. If you can't get the results you want using fully automatic exposure control in difficult lighting situations such as these, using aperture priority or shutter priority modes can prove useful.

Metering Systems

A digital camera uses built-in light meters to measure the light reflecting off the subject. There are several different ways in which the camera's metering mechanism calculates exposure. The metering mode you choose will depend on the particular shot you're taking.

- *Matrix metering*: works by dividing the frame into a grid or matrix. Then it analyzes light at different points on the grid and chooses an exposure that best captures both the dark and light sections of the scene.
- *Centre-weighted metering*: measures light throughout the scene but gives greater importance (weight) to the centre quarter of the image area, assuming that that is where the primary subject is located.
- *Bottom-weighted metering*: measures light throughout the scene but gives greater importance to the bottom of the image area.
- *Spot metering*: measures the light only at the centre of the image. If your background is much brighter than your subject, such as in a backlit situation, spot metering will provide satisfying results.

Exposure Compensation

To gain creative control of exposure, you can use exposure compensation, which is also known as exposure value (EV). Exposure compensation allows you to increase or decrease the exposure from what the autoexposure setting typically delivers.

The settings are different from camera to camera, but usually they appear as +2, +1, –1 and –2, with zero representing the default autoexposure setting. To obtain a brighter image, in a backlit situation for example, you 'dial up', using a positive value to increase the exposure. For a darker image, choose a negative value, thereby decreasing exposure. You might choose a negative value when photographing a scene on a sandy beach. Exposure compensation lets you choose the exposure that is most likely to produce the results you're seeking.

Even by previewing your shots with an LCD screen, you can wind up with disappointing results. Your LCD screen does not provide a 100 per cent accurate representation of your image. Your actual image may be lighter or darker than it appeared when you previewed it.

It takes a lot of practice to get to the point where you know when to lighten or darken a scene. One feature of a digital camera that makes it easier is the LCD screen – because it lets you preview your shot, you don't have to guess whether or not the exposure needs adjusting.

One way to avoid a poorly exposed image is to use a trick that professional photographers often employ. It's called bracketing. The bracketing process means that you take three shots: one at the recommended exposure setting; a second shot that's lighter; and a third shot that's darker, thereby bracketing the recommended exposure with two additional shots. By taking a series of shots at different exposures, you're far more likely to obtain one that's to your liking.

Aperture Priority and Shutter Priority Modes

Using exposure compensation, you can lighten or darken pictures. But to be even more creative, you may want to have more control over the shutter speed and aperture settings. Doing this, you can control the effect of motion and depth of field on your images.

Selecting aperture priority mode gives you control of the aperture. You set the aperture, frame the shot and then press the shutter button halfway to set the focus and exposure. At this point, the camera analyzes what aperture you have chosen and selects the corresponding shutter speed that will result in a well-exposed image. In the same way, when you select shutter priority mode, you decide on the shutter speed and the camera sets the correct aperture.

Exposure compensation control lets you correct exposure. Here are some typical settings and how they are used:

- *+2:* used when there is high contrast between light and dark areas in a scene.
- *+1:* used with sidelit or backlit scenes, such as snow scenes, beach scenes or sunsets.
- *0:* good for evenly lit scenes.

- *−1:* good for scenes where the background is darker than the objects in front of it, such as when an individual is standing in front of a brick wall.
- *−2:* used when the background is very dark and takes up a large portion of the image, and you are striving to maintain detail in the brighter areas of the scene.

Autoflash

As discussed in Chapter 8, a camera with a built-in automatic flash gauges the available light and fires the flash if needed. Because every flash has a useful range, the effects of the autoflash will depend on how bright a light it produces and how far the light has to travel. The further away the subject is from the camera, the less light will be reflected back to the camera. Objects closer to the camera will appear lighter than objects in the background.

When you're taking a photo of a scene with multiple subjects at different distances from the camera, the exposure cannot be correct for all of the subjects. Usually those closest to the camera will be properly exposed. The further the subjects are from the camera, the darker they will appear in the picture. In a shooting situation such as this, you will probably want to turn off the automatic flash and use a fill flash or take other actions to insure a properly lighted photo.

Autofocus

As discussed in Chapter 7, most digital cameras with non-interchangeable lenses are either fixed focus or autofocus. A fixed-focus lens is not adjustable. The camera with a fixed-focus lens captures sharp images of any subject within a certain distance from the lens. Objects outside that range will appear blurred.

Sometimes an autofocus camera will also offer focus lock. Using the focus lock, the photographer can centre the subject in the frame, lock the focus, then reframe and take the shot. When taking a shot of a scene with many elements, this can be a useful feature because it allows you to specify which object you want to be in focus.

Autofocus is a more precise and versatile system than fixed focus. Cameras with autofocus automatically adjust the focus depending on the distance of the subject from the camera. The resulting images will be clearer when taken with an autofocus lens.

Adjusting Colour Balance

You've probably heard the terms cool colours and warm colours. In fact, different light sources really do have different colour temperatures, which means they are made up of varying amounts of red, green and blue light. Colour temperature is measured in degrees Kelvin (°K). For instance, a 100W tungsten light bulb measures 2,850°K; noon light measures about 5,500°K; and average daylight comes in at approximately 6,500°K.

When we take a close look at different sources of light, we can distinguish different colours. Have you noticed how your household lamp throws a golden light on your living room, and how fluorescent tubes cast a cooler, greenish light?

Normally, the human eye compensates for different lighting conditions. Film photographers use special films or filters to compensate for different light sources, but most digital cameras automatically adjust for the correct colour temperature. This process is called colour balance or white balance.

Colour balancing determines what combination of red, green and blue light the camera should perceive as pure white under the current lighting conditions. From there, the camera determines how all other colours can be accurately represented.

Shooting a photo at the wrong colour balance is a much bigger problem with a film camera than it is with a digital camera, since it is easy to compensate for colour balance of a digital image by using image-editing software. However, it is worth noting that you will suffer some loss of definition during the editing process.

Usually, the manual settings for colour balance on a digital camera are as follows:

- *Daylight or sunny* (for shooting in bright outdoor light)
- *Cloudy* (for shooting when it is overcast outdoors)
- *Tungsten/incandescent* (for shooting under standard household lights)
- *Flash* (for shooting with the camera's built-in flash)
- *Fluorescent* (for shooting under fluorescent lights).

Some top-end digital cameras allow you to override the automatic colour balance system. Why would you want to adjust the colour balance manually? Because you can sometimes achieve a desirable effect, such as when you're shooting a candlelit dinner scene. By overriding the colour balance feature, you'll be rewarded with a moody image exhibiting a warm glow. Or sometimes the colour balancing system does not remove all unwanted colours. By choosing a different colour balance setting, you may be able to correct such problems, making colours appear truer.

Continuous Mode

With some digital cameras you can snap an entire sequence of photos. These images can be used to make short films for a website or an animated GIF. There are several ways cameras allow you to capture a series of photos, including the following:

- By depressing the shutter, a digital motor drive or burst mode lets you snap picture after picture.
- Time-lapse photography is achieved by taking a sequence of photos at designated intervals.
- Video-recording mode allows you to take low-resolution videos in MPEG or JPEG formats.

Panoramic Mode

Panoramic mode enables you to take snapshots that are wider than they are high. Digital cameras frequently include panoramic mode.

Some cameras simply capture a band across the middle of the image sensor, leaving black (unexposed) bands at the top and bottom of the photo. The preferred method is to create multiple-image panoramas. This is achieved when you take a series of images while slowly turning in a circle. Then the camera uses special panoramic software to 'stitch' the images together, forming one 360-degree panorama. Many digital cameras come with this panoramic stitching software. This software provides a handy tool when you want to shoot three or four photos and stitch them together, to form a city skyline or a coastline scene, for instance.

One such software program is QuickStitch from Enroute Imaging. Because it is made up of only three main screens, it is fairly easy to learn. You can use it to stitch together anything from two to 36 pictures, vertically or horizontally. The program combines overlapping photos to create virtual reality-like panoramic images up to 360 degrees. The panorama can be outputted to a graphics file or a QuickTime VR movie. QuickTime 4 Pro is a suite of software from Apple that plays digitized video, audio and 'virtual reality' movies. When you add your panorama to a QuickTime file, it becomes part of a virtual reality movie with which a user can interact by moving the mouse to pan and zoom over the scene.

Just as with some point-and-shoot cameras, you can find digital cameras that offer a date/time indicator for a permanent record of when the shot was taken. Some are displayed in the image area, while others are hidden in the image file and can only be seen when using software.

Self-Timers/Remote Controls

A self-timer mechanism delays the shutter release for about 10 seconds, allowing you to jump into a picture before the shutter releases. This is a useful feature when you want to take a self-portrait or include yourself in a group shot.

Wireless remote controls make it a little less stressful, allowing you to walk – not run – to get in the shot. Once you're in position, you simply click a button on the remote and the camera snaps the image. Of course, that leaves you with the question of where to hide the remote...

CHAPTER 11

What Makes a Photograph Memorable

In order to take photographs that capture the viewer's attention, you need to know the elements that combine to form visual impact. These include the visual elements of shape, line, pattern and texture; composition; angle of view; colour; and light. Just as an artist uses paint and canvas to create a painting, a photographer has tools at his or her disposal to create a memorable picture.

Shape

As a photographer, you can create dramatic impact by emphasizing shape. One way to do this is to make a single shape the focus of your image, capturing it against an uncluttered, contrasting background. To do so, you may have to get in close to your subject, or change the camera's angle to rid your picture of distracting details.

In more elaborate compositions, shapes become the building blocks of your image. They can mirror each other in form or provide contrast to create balance or tension. In FIGURE 11-1, the photographer chose to shoot upwards, capturing the shapes of the skyscrapers without the distraction of people and cars on the street below.

FIGURE 11-1: The surprising image of sky-scrapers relies on shape for visual interest.

Photo by Elizabeth T. Schoch

Line

Our eyes follow lines. Lines lead the way, showing us direction and distance. Lines define shapes. They can convey action or force. One of the most important uses of line is to lead the viewer to the centre of interest in the photograph.

tips

The great American photographer Ansel Adams once said, 'There are no rules for good photographs, there are only good photographs.' As you're taking photos with your digital camera, be aware of the shapes around you. How can you use them to form an eye-catching image?

Lines are a tool that the photographer uses to create depth in a photograph. A flat, two-dimensional image takes on life when parallel lines recede to a distant point, creating a sense of perspective and beckoning the viewer to the faraway point.

See how the lines of the stream in FIGURE 11-2 draw us into the distance, giving the impression that the stream flows on forever.

FIGURE 11-2: The lines of the stream beckon us into the distance.

Photo by Elizabeth T. Schoch

You can utilize hard-edged lines to create impact, while curving lines suggest a softer, more graceful feeling. When composing a picture with several elements, lines can be used to direct the eyes of the viewer from one form to another. They can link objects usually considered unrelated. And they can provide information about the action in the picture. Frequently, the opposition of curved and straight lines is used to express action.

The S curve is one of the most common and graceful lines used in composition. An S curve often draws the eye past several points of interest. S-curve compositions typically produce a feeling of calm. Look for an S curve when composing a shot.

Other simple geometric shapes can enhance your photo compositions. The strongest of these is the triangle. A triangle in your composition can add effective visual unity to your image. A V shape typically accentuates perspective and pulls the viewer's eye to the focal point of the picture. The C curve can be useful for framing the main element or drawing the viewer's eye into the picture.

Pattern

FIGURE 11-3: The world is full of patterns. We find them when we take the time to look up, down and all around us.

Photo by Janet McCanna

Patterns are formed when lines, shapes or colours are repeated, as in FIGURE 11-3. Typically, a photographer uses patterns to create a sense of harmony. At the same time, other feelings can arise from photographs showing patterns. Because of their strong visual impact, even the slightest suggestion of a pattern can catch our eye, especially when the elements join together by chance. For instance, the photo in FIGURE 11-4 of seagulls flying suggests freedom and lightness.

Patterns are all around us. Once you begin looking for them, you will find them everywhere. The photo in FIGURE 11-5, taken at Chicago's O'Hare Airport, shows a myriad of patterns surrounding the people making their way through the airport. Look for patterns in your own world, and begin experimenting with them to see what effects you can achieve.

Bear in mind that a pattern alone can make for a dull photo. Make sure that a pattern is strong enough to stand alone before you shoot it. Often you'll want to include additional elements to provide visual interest.

FIGURE 11-4: Patterns are everywhere, as this photographer discovered at the beach when she saw these seagulls.

Photo by Elizabeth T. Schoch

In the photo of the airport, the people add interest and also help the viewer understand what he or she is seeing. In the image of the gulls over the water, the lighthouse and the jetty leading to it help to make a more engaging composition.

FIGURE 11-5: Having your camera handy can mean unexpected photo opportunities. Here, the neon lights above an airport's people-mover provide man-made patterns.

Photo by Elizabeth T. Schoch

Texture

FIGURE 11-6: Texture is not just for close-ups. A shot of palm trees in the South Pacific relies on texture to provide visual interest.

Photo by Elizabeth T. Schoch

Texture appeals to our sense of touch. When used in a photograph, texture adds a feeling of realism to the image. You can utilize texture to portray the nature of a surface: rough, smooth, jagged, bumpy and so forth.

Texture gives a three-dimensional sense to an image, causing the elements to be seen as forms. It helps the viewer perceive the heaviness and bulk, softness and hardness, and roughness or smoothness of the objects.

In FIGURE 11-6, the photo taken of a tropical island pond surrounded by palm trees uses texture to convey the lushness of the vegetation that grows in the sultry South Pacific climate.

FIGURE 11-7: A highly textured subject, such as the red rock formation shown here, can result in a dramatic image that makes us want to reach out and feel its roughness.

Photo by Janet McCanna

The shot of the red rock formation in FIGURE 11-7 is all about texture. When viewing the image, we can immediately imagine how the rock would feel beneath our hands.

Composition

The photographer combines the visual elements – shape, line, pattern and texture – to create a picture. He or she may decide to isolate one element or use a combination of any or all of them.

As a digital photographer, you need to build, or compose, your image using the visual elements. Unlike a painter, you cannot simply pick and choose your objects, colours or position of each (except when combining elements using image-editing software). But you do have certain options that affect the composition of an image, including the ability to move closer or further away from your subject, to choose how you angle your camera, and to decide whether to shoot from above or below your subject.

FIGURE 11-8: In this picture, the viewer's eye focuses on the tree, then travels to the stark landscape around it.

Photo by Elizabeth T. Schoch

Guidelines to good composition are discussed below. Learn them and experiment with them. See how the resulting images change as you change your approach to a scene. Although it is important to know the rules, don't be afraid to break them when it is advantageous to do so. There is no 'right way' to take a photograph.

Your goal is to create an image that quickly and clearly conveys your intended message. Composition is not a haphazard matter. You will need to analyze the elements in a scene, then adjust them for the effect you are seeking. Sometimes you will isolate a single element for a simple but striking image. At other times you will use a combination of elements to tell your story.

You may decide to go for a symmetrical, harmonious picture, or you may deliberately choose to convey a feeling of disharmony and uneasiness.

Perhaps you will choose one main element to dominate the picture, with lesser elements supporting the focal point. This will prompt the viewer's eyes to lock onto the main element, then travel around the frame, as in FIGURE 11-8. The main element may be larger in scale or brighter in colour than other elements in the picture.

Balance and Imbalance

Although you may think that it is desirable to arrange the elements in a picture symmetrically by placing the main subject in the centre with other elements spaced evenly around it, this is exactly the sort of composition you'll want to avoid – a perfectly symmetrical image can appear rigid and uninspiring. To gain and hold a viewer's interest, an image typically contains two main attributes: tension and movement.

FIGURE 11-9: The light and dark areas of this winter scene create a balanced image that is pleasing to the eye.

Photo by Elizabeth T. Schoch

Balance in a successful image comes from the less obvious: the visual weight given to various elements in a picture. You can obtain this type of balance by using contrast, such as bright colours balanced by muted ones, dark objects balanced by lighter backgrounds, or very detailed objects balanced by open areas (SEE FIGURE 11-9).

Graphic designers and interior decorators know a secret that photographers can adopt for more effective photographs: an uneven number of elements is more pleasing to the eye than an even number. If your composition is too balanced, it will result in a bland picture. One good approach is to set up your shot with one main subject and two supporting elements. The main element may be larger in scale or brighter in colour than other elements in the picture. It is easy to compose with three elements, but two elements generally do not work well because your eye does not know where to rest. The exception is when one element is the main focal point and the other is a supporting element.

The Rule of Thirds

FIGURE 11-10: This picture of palm trees successfully utilizes the rule of thirds.

Photo by Elizabeth T. Schoch

One trusted formula for achieving balance is known as the rule of thirds, and painters have successfully employed it for hundreds of years. To utilize the rule of thirds, do this: as you peer through the viewfinder, imagine lines dividing the image into thirds, both horizontally and vertically. Subjects placed near one of the four intersections formed by the lines gain immediate off-centre emphasis. On the other hand, elements situated at diagonally opposed intersections seem balanced. When subjects are located at three of the intersections, they can form a striking triangular composition. In other pictures, the imaginary lines divide a scene into pleasing two-thirds to one-third proportions.

The rule of thirds can be utilized when photographing all subjects, but it works particularly well when you are shooting a relatively small subject photographed against a large expanse or a plain background.

Another way in which the rule of thirds can prove useful is helping the photographer decide where to place the horizon. You can easily arrange the composition by placing the horizon along one of the frame-dividing lines. For instance, in the photograph of a beach on the Polynesian island of Moorea (FIGURE 11-10), the photographer placed the horizon line one-third of the way up from the bottom of the frame, thereby placing the emphasis on the palm trees stretching into the sky.

Angle of View

By changing your camera angle, you can change the viewpoint of your photos, along with their tone and impact. A scene will change dramatically when it is shot from above or below as opposed to eye level. You may need to get down on the ground to achieve the results you're seeking.

FIGURE 11-11:
An interesting image was created by shooting an ordinary revolving door from above.

Photo by Elizabeth T. Schoch

Because we usually view the world from eye level, photos taken at a normal eye-level angle communicate realism. We give power to objects by shooting them from below, so that they appear to tower over us. By shooting from above, objects become diminished, but the arrangement of objects often becomes more noticeable.

FIGURE 11-11 shows a photo of a revolving door that was shot from above. Imagine how ordinary the picture would have seemed if it had been taken from ground level. But because the photographer used an unusual angle of view, she was rewarded with a striking and eye-catching image.

The angle of view can have a dramatic impact on open landscape images. When you shoot from a low angle, more sky is revealed and the spaciousness of the landscape is emphasized. When you shoot from a high angle, the horizon is positioned near the top of the image and the land seems to stretch out to infinity.

When do I use high or low angles of view?
High or low angles of view can be used to reveal patterns and textures not normally perceived at eye level, simplify a composition, isolate a subject against the sky or a plain background, or eliminate a cluttered environment. When shooting the photo of the sunflower in Figure 2-1 in Chapter 2, the photographer used a low angle of view to isolate his subject against the background of the sky.

Try taking a series of pictures of the same scene from different angles of view. How does the angle of view affect the emphasis of the picture? What is being communicated by each image? As Ansel Adams said, 'A good photograph is knowing where to stand.'

Framing

A simple compositional technique known as framing will help you draw a viewer's attention to your image. A window, a doorway and a tree can all act as frames when positioned around the subject of a photo, as can abstract shapes, shadows and blocks of colour. A frame will direct the viewer's eye to the central element of a picture, but it can also do more than that: it can cover unattractive foregrounds or other distracting details, add depth to a photo and identify the photo's setting. For example, a window can be used effectively to frame a scene.

Colour

Colour determines the mood of a picture. When the predominant colours are warm ones, such as yellow or red, the mood is bright and cheerful. Cooler blues, lavenders and greens can convey a calm and tranquil mood, suggesting a sparkling mountain brook or a leafy glade. Contrasting colours create drama, while dark greys and black evoke a more sombre mood.

As a digital photographer, you can manipulate colour, both when shooting and when working with image-editing software after you've captured the image. While shooting, be tuned in to the colours around you. Simply by moving around and changing your angle of view, you may be able to combine colours to better express the story you want your image to tell.

Colour determines the mood of a picture. Warm colours convey cheerful feelings, while cooler colours communicate relaxation. Contrasting colours are exciting. You can choose to effectively combine many colours in your image, use a controlled palette of just one or two colours, or utilize just a splash of lively colour for impact.

Another way to use colour in photography is to compose your picture to include a brightly coloured object against a subdued background. The colour will draw the viewer's eye to the bright item and make it a focal point, even though it may be relatively small in size.

Take care when framing your shot to note where coloured objects are located. Bright patches of colour in less important parts of the scene will draw the viewer's attention there. Don't overload your images with colourful objects; the result can be a busy image that leaves the viewer feeling slightly uneasy.

Light

The other critical component of a good photo is lighting. A photographer uses light in the same way that an artist uses paint. As we discussed in Chapter 2, light is the source of all colour. All colours combine to form white light. When light strikes an object, some colours are absorbed and others are reflected. For instance, a fire engine looks red because its surface is reflecting red and absorbing all other hues. An object appears white when its surface reflects all colours, and black when its surface absorbs them.

Learning the characteristics of light will help you produce better images. First, you must observe light and learn how to take advantage of its colour, quantity, quality, source and direction to create the right mood for your picture.

The sun is the most common source of illumination. During the course of a day, the sun's light shifts from dawn's soft radiance to harsh midday brightness to the delicate, rosy glow of sunset. Once the sun has set, the night is filled with cool tones. When shooting a city skyline at sunset, the buildings will be tinged with the pinks and lavenders of the twilight sky. But under a midday sun, those same buildings will be starkly lit. Bright, sunny days are good for capturing brilliant images. Overcast days produce more subtle colour combinations. The seasons, too, will change the effect of light upon a subject.

A great photograph requires great lighting. The time of day and the resulting angle of light affect form, contrast, texture and colour. Professionals know the best times to shoot. Here is an overview of how light changes throughout the day.

- *Before dawn:* pink, dreamy light; ideal for shooting bodies of water and landscapes.
- *Dawn:* crisp, golden light reflects on subjects facing east.
- *Early morning:* soft light.
- *Midday:* harsh sunlight; best for shooting monuments, buildings and urban streets.
- *Late afternoon:* warm, golden light; ideal for people and landscapes.
- *Sunset:* beautiful skies, especially the 20 minutes before and after the sun sets.
- *Dusk:* the purple glow in the sky does wonderful things to skylines.
- *Night:* if you're willing to experiment at night, you may get some interesting effects.

When you experiment with light and your digital images, you'll see that the positioning of the main source of light strongly affects the photo. A subject can be lighted in three primary ways: from the front, from the back and from the side.

Photo by Philip Thornberry

Taking a picture with the sun behind you results in frontlighting, which provides an even illumination of your subject and tends to produce natural-looking colours. However, since shadows are cast behind the subject, it can appear rather flat, lacking depth and volume. You can turn this to your advantage when you are shooting, to emphasize patterns and when you want forms to appear as two-dimensional shapes.

Lighting your subject from the side will better convey a three-dimensional form. For most photos, sidelighting is the most effective type of illumination. You can use sidelighting to emphasize texture, especially when the light crosses the surface of your subject at a low angle. It also can be used to emphasize the contours of shapes.

Backlighting, lighting that comes from behind a subject, can be difficult to use correctly, but when properly executed, it can produce dramatic results. With strong light, the subject will turn into a silhouette. With weaker light that is balanced by other light from the front or side of the subject, backlighting may produce an effect that is known as rimlighting, which refers to a slightly darker than normal subject that is circled by a halo of light.

Lighting from above, such as the light emitted by the noonday sun, tends to produce unflattering shadows on both people and scenes. However, sometimes it can be utilized to produce drama, for example when shooting images of urban buildings.

Overcast days provide soft light that reveals more subtle colours and detail. When shooting on a sunny day, you can sometimes capture subjects in open shadow for diffused light that reveals vivid colour usually lost in harsh, direct light.

Sunlight not only changes throughout the day, but also from season to season. By studying these changes, you will learn techniques for effectively tackling the challenges presented by different lighting situations; and you will discover new ways of using your digital camera as a creative tool to express your unique message.

CHAPTER 12

Taking Great Pictures

Anyone can be creative with a digital camera. It's not the camera that's important; it's the photographer. With camera in hand, you will choose what scenes to shoot, when to shoot them and from what vantage point. Let's assume that you've just purchased your camera – you're eager to get started, but you're not sure where to begin. First read the manual that came with your camera, which will act as a map, guiding you along your journey into digital photography.

Getting Ready to Shoot

Once you've read the manual and feel confident that you know how to operate your camera, take a moment to consider the basics of snapping a picture. You'll want to always stand with your feet planted firmly. Hold the camera nice and steady (or use a tripod). Gently take a deep breath and hold it, then slowly squeeze the shutter. For still lifes and landscapes, a tripod will ensure that your photo doesn't come out blurred. A cable release makes it easy to shoot once your camera's attached to the tripod.

Inspiration is all around you; you just have to take the time to look for it. Magazines are an easy and inexpensive resource for the photographer looking to expand his or her horizons. Start with a publication that's known for outstanding photography, such as *Life* or *National Geographic*. It's true that monthly issues of *Life* are not available at newsagents any more, but you can view some of its spellbinding images online at *www.lifemag.com. National Geographic* also offers online galleries at its website, *www.nationalgeographic.com*. Study the composition, lighting and use of colour in each photo. What message was the photographer attempting to convey? What techniques did he or she use to communicate the idea?

Looking for inspiration? Turn to the more than one million images found online at TimePix (*www.thepicturecollection.com*), or log onto picture libraries such as Getty Images (*www.gettyimages.com/imagebank*), which provide stock photographs for magazines, newspapers and books. The Hulton Archive (*www.hultonarchive.com*) is a wonderful source of historical images and those by classic photographers.

Workshops and Classes

Photography workshops are held all over the world, and are a great way to turn holiday time into an experience of learning about and practising photography. You get immediate feedback from the instructor, plus you benefit from the opportunity to interact with others who share your passion. As digital photography grows in popularity, more and more digital photography workshops and classes are springing up.

An abundant source for photography workshops is the Internet – a recent check for 'photography workshops' brought up over 20,000 pages of entries, so you should be able to find something somewhere that suits your style of photography and your pocket.

Another option is to take an online or home-study course in digital photography. A number of photography institutes and courses now offer home-study courses that utilize every kind of medium – CD-ROMs, videotapes, audiotapes and books – to bring the information to you in the comfort of your own home.

Don't forget to look in your own area. There's likely to be a photography class available at your local community college, university or adult education institute. Digital photography is gaining popularity so fast that you should be able to find a way to learn more about it without having to venture far from home. Remember, too, that even though you're working with digital photography, many of the approaches to taking a good photo are exactly the same as with film cameras.

Take cues from today's photographers. Examine their work and see what it is that draws – or offends – you. Just bear in mind that you're looking to learn something and be inspired, not to imitate them.

Taking the Picture

Exploring digital photography should be a joyful experience. After all, photography gives us the opportunity to express our feelings. If you are pursuing photography, you've felt the satisfaction that comes from producing a photograph that works. Effective photos move people. They can make us feel uplifted or dispirited, nostalgic or repulsed, regretful or homesick, serene or agitated. Every picture conveys a message. The trick is to make it the message you intend.

'A photograph never grows old. You and I change, people change all through the months and years, but a photograph always remains the same. How nice to look at a photograph of mother or father taken many years ago. You see them as you remember them. But as people live on, they change completely. That is why I think a photograph can be kind.'

Albert Einstein

Your skill as a photographer will increase the more you practise. Using a digital camera makes it even easier to learn by trial and error. First, you can preview your shot in the LCD screen. If you don't like what you see, simply delete it and try again. Second, you benefit from the instant feedback and are able to make adjustments in lighting, angle of view and composition as necessary. And third, you don't have to spend money on film and processing in order to create dozens of images.

FIGURE 12-1: Not everyone has a beautiful violin like this. But the digital photographer can find other everyday objects that can be transformed into memorable shots.

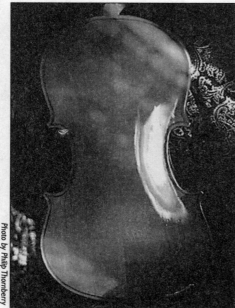

Photo by Philip Thornberry

The first step to being a good photographer is learning to see the world as the camera sees it. When we look around us, we automatically and unconsciously screen out a great deal. Clutter seemingly disappears from our view. Not so with the camera; it will record everything in a scene. As we look at the world, we view it in three dimensions. The camera produces a two-dimensional image. And our eyes adapt to the lighting, but the camera's does not. The photographer learns to recognize and make alterations for these differences.

Take a look around you right now. What do you notice? Good photos can be taken anywhere. And although it would be a grand adventure to travel the globe taking pictures, it is not necessary to venture far from home to capture intriguing images. Seemingly ordinary subjects can make extraordinary photographs, as with the violin in FIGURE 12-1.

An important skill for the photographer is previsualization: the ability to imagine how the photo will look. This only occurs when the photographer understands how the camera 'sees' and how it will capture the image. Previsualization for the digital photographer requires an understanding of composition, light and how a digital camera works.

Where to Begin

Start with your passion. Besides photography, what else do you enjoy? Perhaps you love to play sports, listen to music or collect antiques. Maybe in your spare time you like to read a bestseller, bicycle with your children or dance the night away at a local club. You can combine other interests with your passion for photography, especially when you're using an easily portable digital camera. Next time you're heading for the club, take along your camera. You'll be rewarded with great action shots of people on the dance floor. Bring your camera with you to the next flea market or boot sale, and you'll have a means of recording the treasures you decide to bring home plus the merchandise you didn't buy.

Recording Everyday Life

Don't wait for a special occasion. Start carrying your camera with you wherever you go. You'll get more practice, which will help you move faster towards your aim of being a good photographer, and you'll end up with engaging images you never would have dreamed of taking.

What about carrying your camera to work with you? Even an ordinary working day holds plenty of potential. Don't wait until you reach the office to start shooting. There's no reason you can't take pictures from your seat on the bus or train. If you're commuting by car, you'll need to keep your attention on your driving. But you might be able to shoot out of the car window when you've stopped at a red light. Maybe during your tedious commute you've already entertained yourself by framing certain shots in your mind. Pack your camera in your case or bag tomorrow, and you can start turning those imaginary images into the real thing.

FIGURE 12-2: Walking through a large city, the photographer noticed the strong lines and angles of a building and emphasized them to create a striking image.

Photo by Philip Thornberry

Familiar Faces

Most of us take snapshots on our holidays, but consider taking pictures of your favourite people on a regular basis. Your children, friends and relatives are all potential subjects. Perhaps taking portraits will even become your speciality. (You'll find more tips on portrait photography later in this chapter.)

Capture your loved ones while they are carrying out their daily routines. What about a picture of the baby having her nightly bath? Your nursery-school child would be delighted to have you look over his shoulder while he finger-paints his next masterpiece. And Great Aunt Isabel would probably be flattered if you asked to take a photo of her in her garden next to her prize rose bush.

FIGURE 12-3:
Animals, large or
small, can make
satisfying images.
Taking her
camera to a barn
allowed the
photographer to
capture a young
friend grooming
her horse.

Photo by Elizabeth T. Schoch

Developing a Personal Style

Sooner or later, most photographers find that they are drawn to a
particular subject, such as portraits, landscapes, travel photos and so forth.
As you take more and more photos, you will develop a personal style that
will become increasingly apparent in your images. You may find yourself
attracted to certain subjects or techniques. Although it is helpful to study
the styles of other photographers, it is not necessary to imitate them. Your
own style will develop naturally. Don't force it. Just enjoy the process, and
you are bound to find your individual approach to digital photography.

Don't force yourself to choose a speciality. It isn't necessary, and it isn't
advisable. Just experiment and see where your photography leads you.
This is about being creative and having fun, not fitting into any particular
mould or following any rules.

Little Things Mean a Lot

A good photographer pays attention to details in order to be rewarded with excellent images. Remember these tips for better digital pictures:

· When shooting people, get close to your subject. People make better subjects when they're interacting than when they stand stiffly.
· Closer is better. Many mediocre shots would have been impressive if the photographer had only moved closer to the subject.
· Use flash outdoors to eliminate shadows.
· Avoid wide-angle distortion.
· Do not centre all your pictures in the frame. Use the focus-lock feature on your camera to avoid this problem.
· Partial images can be very dramatic. Shoot close-ups or crop your photos to provide interesting images.
· Avoid excessive compression of your digital images. You lose detail each time an image is compressed.
· At night, turn off the autoflash and use a tripod for better images.
· Image-editing software is a great tool, but it will never replace a good photographer. You want to think about the composition as you're setting up a shot.

Time and Its Effect on Photographs

Time can have a profound effect on photographs. The following sections examine some of the relationships between time and the images captured by photographers.

The Decisive Moment

There are many ways in which time can influence photography. The great photographer Henri Cartier-Bresson (1908–2004) was a proponent of a technique known as the decisive moment. This term refers to his belief that in every event there is a specific moment when all the elements combine to create an image that tells the full story of that moment. In his book, *The Decisive Moment*, he wrote: 'A velvet hand, a hawk's eye – these we should all have.... If the shutter was released at the decisive moment, you have instinctively fixed a geometric pattern without which the photograph would have been both formless and lifeless.'

FIGURE 12-4: This photo of a diver illustrates Henri Cartier-Bresson's famous decisive moment technique, where a single moment in time tells a complex story.

Photo by Philip Thornberry

Action Shots

Another way in which time influences a photo is when the photographer freezes the action or captures movement. Action shots bring to mind pictures taken at sporting events, but you can record any movement or action and create a memorable image. If you've ever captured the action of your son's football match or your daughter's tennis games, you've experienced the relationship of time and photography.

Time and Nature

When we view scenes of the natural world, we are also seeing the effects of time on the environment. Photos taken in different seasons remind us that although seasons change, and the landscape changes with them, the serenity of the natural world remains.

You don't need to go far to witness the effect of time on the environment. Simply look out of the window to discover seasonal changes in your own garden, or take a walk to a nearby park. As a photographic exercise, consider taking a series of shots of a particular outdoor scene to record the ways in which it changes with the seasons.

Time and People

Because time affects people too, we glimpse time when we view pictures of children, teenagers, adults and older people. When subjects of different generations are photographed together, we are especially struck by the cycle of life. During the course of our busy days, we don't often stop to reflect on the ways in which time changes us. Seeing a photograph can make us pause and consider the passage of time.

CHAPTER 13

Types of
Photographs

Some photographers enjoy taking specific types of photos, including portraits, landscapes, still lifes, nature scenes and urban subjects. In this section, we will examine some of the different subjects that people like to photograph and the best ways to capture them as digital images.

Portraits

People are the most popular subjects for photographers. A truly good portrait conveys something about the subject's personality. When taking portraits, you're going to have to gain the subject's cooperation in order to capture a good image.

When photographing your family and friends, avoid stiff, posed pictures. Don't make your subjects stand awkwardly facing the camera. Place them in a natural, comfortable position. Allow them to sit or lean against something so they will feel, and look, more relaxed. Usually, you'll want to make eye contact to create a feeling of intimacy. Get close and concentrate on the person's head rather than their entire body.

If your subject is looking right at the camera, be careful that he or she is not squinting into the sun. Change your shooting position, or try to find a bit of open shade so that he or she can look away from the sun. Use a fill flash to avoid shadows on the subject's face.

When taking pictures of children, get down to their level for a better angle of view. You may want to forego posing them. Instead, wait until they're involved in an activity, then catch them at play.

Regardless of whether you're photographing kids or adults, warm up with some 'practice' shots so that everyone involved gets used to the camera and relaxes a bit.

When shooting indoors, turn on your camera's red-eye reduction mode or the overhead lights, or get the subject to look at a light before you take the picture. These techniques help avoid that scary red-eye syndrome.

Taking Better Portraits

Because we so often want to capture our loved ones in pictures, you may find it useful to review the following pointers on taking portraits:

· Never shoot directly into the light.
· Take some warm-up shots to give your subjects a chance to relax.

· Consider using props that convey your subject's personality.
· Get close to your subject.
· Avoid the red-eye effect when using the flash.
· Remember that you may not be able to quickly take a series of photos due to shutter lag.
· You may want to use a tripod to steady the camera, especially when shooting in low light.
· Candids typically catch people with more natural facial expressions than posed shots.
· Allow children time to become absorbed in what they are doing before you take the photo.

The American photographer Annie Leibovitz (b. 1949) is recognized for her portraits. For the last 25 years her work has appeared in a number of magazines, including *Rolling Stone*, *Vogue* and *Vanity Fair*, and she has had one-woman exhibitions at art and photography galleries across the world. Her portrait of John Lennon on a bed with Yoko Ono is one of Leibovitz's best-known works and is also the last formal portrait of the Beatle before his death. Her book *Women* includes portraits of women from diverse backgrounds, including actresses, a soldier, miners, showgirls and farmers. Leibovitz says, 'In a portrait, you have room to have a point of view and to be conceptual with a picture. The image may not be literally what's going on, but it's representative.'

Candids

Candid shots can be marvellous. Catch the action when people are involved in an activity.

In these instances you can get a good shot without making your subjects stop and face the camera. If you're outdoors, the people you're photographing may be looking around at the scenery and you can catch them enjoying the view.

If you carry your camera with you wherever you go, you'll find plenty of opportunities to shoot candid shots of strangers. You'll need to be prepared to act quickly to make the most of spontaneous photo opportunities. Candid shots can reveal far more than posed portraits, since they catch people unaware and thus looking more natural. When taking a candid shot on a busy urban street or in the middle of a gathering, timing is crucial for success. A good candid requires capturing the decisive moment that Henri Cartier-Bresson talked about. Your goal is to capture the one specific moment that tells the full story of that moment.

One good way to approach candid photography is to make yourself invisible during the process. Perhaps you can find a corner at a party where you can unobtrusively sit and wait for the right time to shoot. Or you can take a more active approach by walking through a busy urban area with camera in hand, looking for interesting subjects among the people shopping, strolling and hurrying to and from work.

Some people are not going to welcome your taking their picture. Avoid anyone who looks unfriendly, and be ready to explain what you are doing if anyone questions you.

You'll need a fairly good optical zoom on your digital camera to be able to remain removed from your subject while shooting. Remember to turn off your flash.

Pets

Man's best friends are also popular subjects for photos. We think of our pets as members of our families, so it's not surprising that we love to include their images in our photo albums. Candid shots work especially well, since it is hard to keep your dog or cat sitting to attention for very long. You can try using a squeaky toy to draw their attention towards the camera, or wait and snap a candid shot the next time a family member is playing with your dog or cat. For dogs, move outdoors for some good action shots, such as catching a Frisbee in the park or running along a beach.

Those who want to photograph pets can find inspiration in the photography of William Wegman, who is known for dressing up his Weimaraners and using them as models in his photographs. His images of his dog, Man Ray, and three other Weimaraners appear in books and on posters, T-shirts, calendars, magnets, mouse pads and more. His website *(www.wegmanworld.com)* tells how he began photographing dogs and why he has continued to do it for the last 20 years or so.

Although cats and dogs are the most popular household pets, don't overlook the hamster, bird or gerbil that calls your house home. Even the smallest animal can feature in your photography plans.

Landscapes

An imaginative photographer can create a beautiful landscape, whether he or she is visiting the North Yorkshire Moors or the tropical island of Tahiti. Landscapes are simply photos that portray an outdoor place, regardless of its location.

When confronted with a scenic vista, many photographers are inclined to use a wide-angle lens to capture as much of the view as possible. However, it can be better to use a telephoto lens to zero in on an especially interesting portion of a scene. Regardless of your approach, you should attempt to present your landscapes with as little clutter as possible.

Your aim when photographing a landscape is to capture the spirit of the place. What is it about the scene that attracts you? Perhaps it's the late-afternoon sunlight shining on the ocean waves as they lap the shoreline. Maybe it's the cloud shadows on the mountains beyond the forest. Light has a dramatic effect on landscapes, as does weather. Be aware that the quality of light, like the weather, is constantly changing. You must shoot quickly if you wish to capture that setting sun or those dark storm clouds that will soon deliver rain. See FIGURES 13-1, 13-2 and 13-3 for some dramatic landscape images.

FIGURE 13-1: By photographing the Irish countryside from above, the photographer created a pleasing image that relies on soft shapes and rich colours for visual impact.

Photo by Philip Thornberry

FIGURE 13-2: Natural scenes evoke a gamut of emotions; maybe that is why so many photographers are drawn to the outdoors.

Photo by Philip Thornberry

You don't have to be a student of landscape photography to recognize the name Ansel Adams. His powerful black-and-white images capturing the loveliness and majesty of the American western landscape are frequently seen on calendars and posters and in books. A visionary who understood the importance of protecting the environment, Adams spent some of his early years photographing the Yosemite Valley, an experience that provided lifelong inspiration. Adams is known for his development of the Zone System, a classification of his approach to exposure, processing and printing.

The Zone System was based on the concept of previsualization, the ability to imagine how the finished photo will look given a particular set of conditions. The Zone System provided a means of controlling the optical, mechanical medium of photography with adroitness, similar to the way an artist wields a brush and paints. Adams's legendary technical genius enabled him to take an ordinary scene and transform it into a radiant photograph.

FIGURE 13-3: This photograph of a beautiful lake in Ireland emphasizes the spaciousness of the landscape.

Photo by Philip Thornberry

Panoramas

Sometimes nothing else will do but to capture a panoramic image of a scene. Use the panoramic mode on your camera to take a picture of that sweeping vista. Panoramic shots are especially appropriate for subjects such as city skylines, seascapes, mountains and bridges.

When shooting in panoramic mode, watch the edges of the viewfinder to be sure you include only what you really want.

 Take care to keep the horizon level near the middle of the frame. If you don't, the horizon will bend, either upwards (if the horizon is too low) or downwards (if it is too high).

If you have panoramic software that allows you to 'stitch' images together, you can take a series of images while slowly turning in a circle. Then the camera uses the software to form one 360-degree panorama. Many digital cameras come with this panoramic stitching software.

Sunsets

Few people can resist the splendour of a spectacular sunset. To catch all the glorious colour, you must be prepared to work quickly. Take a series of shots and vary your position. In some photos, include elements in the foreground. In others, fill the frame with sky. Remember that the colourful sky is really what you are trying to capture, so even after the sun sinks beneath the horizon you can continue shooting and end up with some good, interesting images.

Still Lifes

Although fruit or flowers may be the first things that come to mind when you hear the words 'still life', just about anything can qualify as a subject. A still life simply refers to an inanimate object, or group of objects, composed and captured in an interesting way. For centuries, painters have used still lifes to explore their craft, and photographers can do the same.

When photographing a still life, you have complete control over the creative process and can experiment with shape, light, colour, texture and composition. Still lifes tend to be more time-consuming because you must first set up the shot. By paying attention to detail and allowing your creativity to surface, you can create a memorable still-life image.

Many of the photographs used in advertising are still lifes. Open a magazine and study the ads for clues as to what works and what doesn't. Notice what draws your eye, paying attention to the use of lighting, colour, composition, shapes and texture. You will see that photographers use techniques such as patterns (repetition of shapes and lines), a combination of complementary or clashing colours and a focus on one main object when creating noteworthy still-life images.

When setting up your own still life, everyday items you have around the house can be used to make a statement if they're arranged well. To make it more than just a snapshot, you will need to consider the texture, theme and composition of your image. Your choices of subject, position and lighting will be the keys to creating successful still-life images.

Pick objects of complementary or contrasting colour or shape, things that will work together to convey a story, or objects that are found together in nature. Arrange them so that they are leaning against or are placed next to each other. Larger items will become the main focal points of the composition, with smaller objects placed in front of them.

Vary the lighting for different effects, but consider your subject and the outcome you are trying to create. Soft, diffuse lighting will give the image a soft quality, like a painting. Stronger light is more appropriate for use with a still life composed of contemporary or angular items. Varying the angle of the light also changes the mood of the shot. Lighting your still life from above will make it appear more grounded. If you light it from below, the objects will cast high shadows and appear larger.

When shooting indoors, you may want to take a tip from the professionals and create backdrops for your still life. Any solid-colour cloth can be used, as can professional seamless background paper that is available in a variety of colours and textures.

When working outdoors, you'll probably use natural lighting to complement objects found in nature. Try shooting in open shade for best results. If extra light is required, bounced flash lighting or a photo reflector will add more light to the scene.

Edward Weston (1886–1958), considered one of the great masters of 20th-century photography, began taking pictures seriously at the age of 16, and had his first photography exhibition while still a teenager. He is particularly known for his classic black-and-white nudes, portraits, natural landscapes and still lifes of peppers, shells, stones and rocks.

Weston used large-format cameras and available light to create sensuous images of lyrical beauty. He was a contemporary of Ansel Adams, Alfred Stieglitz, Paul Strand and Georgia O'Keeffe. Edward Weston was a founding member of Group f/64, a group of purist photographers that was established in 1932 and included Adams. Of Weston's photographs, Adams said, 'His work illuminates man's inner journey toward perfection of the spirit.'

Silhouettes

You can create interesting images with silhouettes. A silhouette is an outline of a subject filled in with black or a dark colour and set against a lighter background.

Capturing a silhouette is not particularly hard. The light must be behind the subject you want to silhouette so that you are, in effect, underexposing the subject.

Silhouettes have the most impact when you incorporate an opaque object and a bright background. Look for a bold subject with a simple shape, one that the viewer can easily recognize. The background can be any light-coloured expanse, such as the sunset sky, the glittering sea or even a pale-coloured building.

To get the best exposure, turn your viewfinder towards the brightest area of the scene, then lock in the exposure and reframe the shot. If your camera has exposure compensation, take a reading of the bright area, then bracket the shot so you can subsequently choose the image with the exposure that you like best.

Cities

The movement, colour and exuberance of city streets make them an ideal place for taking photos. Amid the urban commotion you'll find all matter of subjects, including eye-catching architecture, captivating faces, lush public parks and gardens, fountains, green markets and historic landmarks. Even public urban transport – taxis, buses and underground trains – can be inspiration for your digital images.

Whether you live in the city or are just visiting, take a walk to really get a feel for its flavour. You'll be part of the general hustle and bustle, so you'll be able to spot interesting details as you stroll around. Think about what you'd like to shoot. Are you looking for anything that grabs your attention, or do you have a particular subject in mind?

If you're in a city with a long history, look for opportunities to show the old and the new side by side. For instance, if you're visiting central London, a shot of Christopher Wren's St Paul's Cathedral surrounded by contemporary glass office blocks would show an interesting juxtaposition of the historic and the modern.

For a different perspective on a city, you might want to get above or beyond the action. If you look down on streets, they become lines forming interesting patterns. For a good vantage point, see if the city offers an observation tower. Or if you're staying in a high-rise hotel, you may be able to shoot photos from your room.

You may need to get away from the city to get an expansive view. To shoot from the water, take a boat or ferry ride. Even a bridge, such as the High Level Bridge in Newcastle, can offer a fantastic place from which to photograph a city.

Cities and towns can lack a little lustre at midday, but in the evening they take on a glamorous glow. Try shooting at twilight, when there is lots of blue light left in the sky, and see how the buildings glimmer. Just before sunset you can shoot from the west to catch the setting sun lighting up the skyline – especially when captured in dramatic evening light, skylines can make breathtaking images.

When taking pictures at dusk or dawn, it becomes difficult for your digital camera to judge the right exposure. Take a series of shots so you'll be guaranteed satisfying results.

Turn your travel images into a slide show, and you can share your exciting adventures with everyone you know. With a digital camera and the right software, you can produce a show that bears little resemblance to the proverbial sleep-inducing slide shows of the past.

Just like your trip, your show should have a beginning, middle and end, and ideally it will include a variety of close-ups, panoramas and wide-angle shots.

When visiting metropolitan areas, walk through busy districts with your camera in hand. Keep your eyes open for interesting subjects, such as people shopping or making their way to work, and architectural details that will convey the mood of the place.

Open-air markets, with their colourful produce stands, merchandise vendors and shoppers haggling for the best bargains, can be fodder for your photographs. Urban parks can reveal lovely fountains and gardens, while skyscrapers can be used to produce striking graphic images.

If your trip takes you to a tropical destination, the beaches, luscious flowers and colourfully garbed people can all combine to spark your imagination. When travelling by cruise ship, you'll have all sorts of opportunities to get photos, both on board the ship and when stopping at ports of call. You can shoot scenery from the deck of the ship, capture the impressions of the island markets and even record the action at the ship's buffet table or dance floor.

When combined into one slide show, a medley of images can provide a wonderful view of the places you've seen.

Architectural Details

FIGURE 13-4: There are many ways in which architectural details can be captured. An elaborate lighting fixture in a bank provided the photographer with inspiration for this photo.

Photo by Janet McCanna

Although it is fun to capture the magnificence of a famous structure, such as Windsor Castle or the Eiffel Tower, many buildings offer subtle architectural details that make exquisite images on their own. Menacing gargoyles, centuries-old weathervanes and luminescent stained-glass windows are just some of the compelling details that can be used to create whimsical photos.

A building's many details combine to give the structure its architectural style. Think of the elaborate gingerbread of a Victorian house, the stainless-steel exterior of an Art Deco restaurant and the fluted columns of a Greek Revival town hall – all details that immediately declare the style of the building.

FIGURE 13-5: Although there are many photos of St Patrick's Cathedral in New York, here the photographer chose to show just this elaborate door.

Photo by Elizabeth T. Schoch

The best photos of architectural details are those that are tightly composed so the subject fills the frame. Depending on how far you are from your subject, you may be able to use a normal lens or moderate telephoto. If you are too far away, you'll need a more powerful telephoto lens. Be sure to note the lighting – ideally, it will be coming from the side so that texture and details will be readily revealed. If you are concerned about capturing colour, a hazy day will offer the most saturated hues.

If you're interested in shooting architectural details, begin by taking the time to look for them. Although you may first think of visiting cathedrals and historic structures, remember that even a simple country barn or town house can offer interesting shapes and patterns. As you begin to become more and more aware of the details of the buildings around you, you may be surprised at how many can be used effectively in your digital images. FIGURES 13-4 and 13-5 show some of the many ways that architectural details can be captured with a camera.

Close-Ups

If your digital camera has a close-up mode, you can enjoy taking intimate shots of the world around you. Nature offers a limitless array of possibilities, from an elegant butterfly perched on a garden bush to tidal pools hidden among seaside rocks. Even in your own home, anything can be a possible subject for a close-up, from a coin in the palm of your hand to a pile of paper clips on a desk.

If you can select the aperture on your camera, use the minimum aperture when taking close-ups to provide as much depth of field as possible. Getting the right light can be tricky, and you may get better results if you turn off the flash and use available lighting. Make sure you aren't throwing a shadow onto your subject. Use a tripod to avoid camera shake.

Good Pictures Are Everywhere

You need not be a globetrotter to take impressive photos. Start in your own back garden, or take a walk down the streets near where you live. The great photographer Edward Steichen (1879–1973) took hundreds of pictures of a tree near his home in Connecticut. 'Each time I look at these pictures,' he said, 'I find something new there. Each time I get closer to what I want to say about that tree.'

Photography Log

It is very easy to forget the details of an image you've taken. Here is a log to help you record all the pertinent information about your photos.

Frame	Date	Aperture	Shutter speed	Lens	Notes
0					
1					
2					
3					
4					
5					
6					
7					
8					
9					
10					
11					
12					
13					
14					
15					
16					
17					
18					
19					
20					
21					
22					
23					
24					

CHAPTER 14

Downloading Images

Downloading refers to the transfer of images from your camera's storage media to a storage device located on a computer, printer or other device. Downloading is accomplished by connecting the camera directly to the computer using a cable, or removing the media from the camera and inserting it into a special drive. You can also utilize wireless technology to make the transfer.

Connecting Your Camera With Cable

You can connect your camera to your computer or other device in several ways. Most digital cameras come with software and a transfer cable. To transfer images, you insert the cable into a port on your computer. The type of port your computer uses will determine the length of time it will take you to download your images.

Usually, the process of transferring image files from your camera to a computer using a USB or serial port begins with the downloading of the thumbnails for each file. The thumbnails take the place of a contact sheet, allowing you to view your images. Using the thumbnails, the photographer decides what files to download and what files to delete.

Typically, the transfer process happens in this way:

1. Using the computer, open the camera's software.
2. Open the picture files.
3. Choose the ones you want to transfer to the computer.
4. Select the directory to which you'd like to transfer the files.
5. Select 'Transfer selected images'.
6. The downloading process begins.

When downloading images without a memory card reader, you'll save your battery power if you plug your camera into an electrical outlet using the camera's charger. Because downloads can take several minutes, using the charger will keep you from draining your camera's batteries.

Serial Ports

When digital point-and-shoot cameras were first introduced, the only way to download pictures from the camera's memory to a computer was to connect the camera directly to the computer using a serial cable. Today serial ports are generally used for connecting analogue modems so that the user can access the Internet. But some digital cameras still use serial ports to connect to a computer. A serial cable transmits information one bit of data at a time, which makes for a very slow process, however.

The upside of using a serial port is that almost every computer has one (except Macs), so any camera can be downloaded to any computer. The downside is the extremely slow transfer rate of the serial connection, which is limited to 150–230 kilobits per second (Kbps). The other drawback is that you have to have your computer to hand in order to download your stored images to it.

Downloading using a serial cable is the slowest way to transfer images to a computer. It takes about five or six minutes to download 8MB of images. To download your images using a serial cable, you'll need special software, and glitches can occur during the transfer process.

Parallel Ports

Faster than serial ports, parallel ports can carry 8 bits of data at a time. They are normally used for printers and certain kinds of external storage devices. Many card readers plug into a parallel port.

SCSI Ports

SCSI (which stands for Small Computer System Interface) connections transfer data at a rate of 40Mbps (megabits per second) to 640Mbps. Used by Macintosh computers more than PCs, SCSI is fast, but it has certain drawbacks. Before you start your computer, you must connect and turn on the SCSI device. Although a SCSI port can accommodate up to seven devices, they must be 'daisy-chained' by plugging one device into another. SCSI requires a bit of patience to utilize, as it's a fairly complex method of connection and can be difficult to operate.

If you need a fast and easy way to connect a SCSI device to a USB-equipped PC or Macintosh computer, try the USBXchange from Adaptec, which even includes an adapter for the larger classic SCSI connector. See their website, *www.adaptec.com*, for more information.

USB Connections

Computers manufactured after around 1998 typically have a USB connection. Downloading via the USB is a much faster and easier way to transfer your images than using a serial cable. USB can transfer images at up to 12Mbps, which is about 50 times faster than the fastest serial connection. Downloading 8MB of images via USB should take you less than one minute. If your computer has a USB, you may want to purchase a USB-compatible digital camera.

In addition to saving you time when you download, another great advantage to using a USB camera is that it's hot-swappable, which is just a fancy way of saying that you don't have to turn off the computer or the camera when you plug or unplug the camera from the USB port. With USB, you can daisy-chain up to 127 devices on a single USB port, which makes it easy for you to custom-build a system. You can use USB with CD-ROM drives, hard drives and video equipment.

FireWire

Even faster than a conventional serial bus port is FireWire, a high-speed, high-performance serial bus. FireWire was introduced by Apple in their Power Macs, but today it is used throughout the electronics industry. (FireWire is the name patented by Apple, but it is also referred to as IEEE 1394 and i.LINK.)

The FireReaders line of card readers from FirewireDirect allows the user to plug the reader into a PC's FireWire port for operation. It comes in models for CompactFlash and Secure Digital versions. Each allows hot-swapping so the user is able to replace cards without restarting the computer. The reader is designed for use with digital cameras, MP3 players, PDAs and other devices.

FireWire transfers data from a computer to another device very quickly – at 100, 400 or 600Mbps – fast enough for digital camera images and uncompressed digital video. It is pretty well accepted that FireWire is quickly becoming the data transmission standard of the digital world. FireWire is easy to use and is hot-swappable. It permits up to 63 devices, such as digital cameras, digital camcorders, music devices, printers and scanners, to be connected to one port.

FireWire is compatible with Apple PowerBook G3 and PowerMac G4 computers, iMacs and eMacs, Compaq 5600 Series desktop computers, several Kodak DCS digital cameras, the Sony Vaio, Canon's Optura Pi digital-video camera, the Canon EOS D2000 and the Nikon D1 digital camera, and new compatible models are introduced frequently.

 It's easy for computer users to accumulate a mass of power and linking cables, with computer, monitor, mouse and keyboard all needing to be connected. Label your power and connecting cables each time you install hardware, to avoid having to work out what each piece does.

Downloading Directly From Storage Media

Even faster than USB or serial transfers are downloads that work with removable storage media such as CompactFlash and Secure Digital. Listed below are some of the options if your camera uses removable media.

Memory Card Readers

Memory card readers are available from a number of different manufacturers. They not only help you to transfer digital images from cameras quickly and simply, but they also work with MP3 players, PDAs and the Internet. The readers work with Secure Digital, CompactFlash xD and other memory cards, allowing users to copy and move digital files from one device to another. A memory card reader plugs into a serial, parallel or USB port. A growing number of card readers also utilize FireWire ports.

Floppy Disks and Floppy Disk Adapters

If your camera uses a floppy disk as storage media, you simply remove the disk from your camera and insert it into your computer. It couldn't be easier. Of course, there are drawbacks to floppy disks: (1) the camera must be big enough to accommodate the floppy disk, and (2) a floppy disk holds only up to 1.5MB of data, which is much less than flash memory cards.

If you wish to use removable storage media with your floppy drive, you can purchase a FlashPath adapter, which is shaped like a floppy disk and inserts into the standard drive slot found on almost all computers. You can then insert the media card into the FlashPath and begin downloading images. You won't need a cable connection to utilize the FlashPath adapter, but you will need driver software. FlashPath adapters are available for SmartMedia and some other cards.

PC Card Adapters

You'll typically find a PC card port on notebook PCs, PowerBooks and some handheld devices. If your computer supports Type II cards, you can purchase a PC card adapter for either CompactFlash or SmartMedia. Then it's a simple process of inserting your flash memory card into the adapter and plugging the adapter into your PC. The great thing about using a PC card adapter is that it's immediately ready to use – there's no driver or other software necessary. The downloading process is really fast: you can copy 8MB of images in just a few seconds. The PC card appears as a drive on the computer desktop, and you simply drag and drop image files from the PC card to the hard drive.

Memory card readers are great for downloading digital images because you don't have to hook the camera to the computer. By inserting your card into the reader, you're ready to access image files. Once the memory card is full, you can download it using the reader and keep on taking pictures.

ImageMate Drive

SanMate manufactures the ImageMate Drive, an external CompactFlash drive that allows you to transfer image files from your camera at a rate 40 times faster than a serial cable connection. It connects to your computer using either a USB or parallel port. Once you've got it hooked up, it appears on your desktop as a drive so you can easily drag and drop files from your digital camera. It also works for downloading files from handheld computers and the Internet.

Iomega PocketZip Drive

If you're a photographer who likes to travel, you may be interested in Iomega's PocketZip. The compact, rechargeable, handheld drive can read CompactFlash and SmartMedia cards, among others. PocketZip then automatically transfers the images to 100MB disks smaller than a CD. Once you're back at home, you simply connect the PocketZip drive to your computer's parallel port for downloading to your hard drive.

PocketZip disks provide an economical alternative to 32MB solid-state memory cards, which retail for a great deal more and provide only one-third the capacity. If you plan to spend a day shooting photos on location, you may want to investigate the PocketZip drive.

Wireless Transfers

Wireless is quickly becoming the way to go. And now you can transfer your digital images using wireless technology.

Infrared Transfer

You can avoid the hassle of connecting your camera to your computer with cables by using wireless infrared (IrDA). You'll need a digital camera with an IrDA port and a receiving device that also features this technology, such as another digital camera, a computer or a printer.

IrDA wireless transfer utilizes infrared light beams to carry files. This same technology has been used for more than 20 years in television and VCR remote controls. Many devices today feature IrDA ports, including digital cameras, notebook computers, mobile phones, digital pagers, printers, PDAs, organizers, PC card adapters and others. Some digital camera manufacturers who utilize IrDA technology are Casio, Sharp, Kodak and Sony. If your computer does not have infrared capability, you can buy an adapter that plugs into one of its ports and allows it to be used with your IrDA-equipped camera.

To transfer your image files, just put your camera near your computer or other IrDA-equipped device and begin the transfer process. The downloading speed will be determined by the capabilities of the receiving device's IrDA port.

Mobile Phones

How about skipping the step of downloading to your computer altogether? You can send and receive digital pictures over the Internet using a growing number of mobile phones. This platform has been designed to enable users to quickly and effortlessly share digital photographs.

A photographer using mobile phone connected to an iDEN (Integrated Digital Enhanced Network) link can capture, send and receive images wirelessly. The process allows the transmittal of digital images via the Internet to friends, family and colleagues anywhere in the world.

The combination is ideal for anyone wanting to quickly capture images and transmit them immediately. In effect, it allows you to use an Internet-ready iDEN mobile phone as a modem for your camera. You can post images on any website, including your own business or personal site or a photo-sharing site where others may view your pictures. The link automatically sends an e-mail containing the link to your photos. You can also download pictures from your mobile phone into your computer via a standard USB port and cable.

The mobile phone industry is even faster-developing than the digital camera one, and today's latest model will undoubtedly be obsolete within a year or so – but at time of writing, some companies' phones – such as Sharp, Sony and Ericsson and the Nokia 6030 – can produce images with 256,000 colours, compared to under 10,000 only a couple of years ago. The quality is not as high as that of a good compact digital camera, but the ease of use and low cost (with a standard mobile phone contract, many camera phones come free) makes them a handy and very portable alternative.

Other Types of Transfers

Your digital camera can also be connected to a television, VCR or printer. Let's examine how you can transfer images to these types of equipment.

Connecting to a Television or VCR

If your camera has a video-out mini-jack socket, you can use this to connect to a TV using standard input or video-in terminals. This type of connection allows you to view your images on your TV or record them on videotape using your VCR, or to DVD via some DVD writers.

When you display your images on a TV screen, you can see them a lot more easily and clearly than when you view them on a computer monitor. Because of the bigger screen, small imperfections become more readily discernible. If you have a group of people who would like to see your images, whether for business purposes or just for fun, this is one way to do it.

By recording your images on video you can create your own slide show, complete with sound if your camera provides the ability to record audio.

A word of warning: older cameras sold in the USA output video in NTSC format, the format used by TVs in North America. British and European televisions use the PAL format, so you won't be able to display digital images from such an American camera on your TV unless your camera has PAL capability. Newer digital cameras offer the choice of NTSC or PAL formats.

To transfer images between your digital camera and a TV, in most cases you connect one end of an AV cable to the camera's video-out or AV-out jack and the other to your TV or VCR's video-in jack. If your camera has the ability to record audio, you will use a separate AV plug for the audio signal, inserting it into the audio-in jack.

Be aware that your camera's software must allow you to transfer downloaded images back to the camera or you will lose your images unless you record them on video.

Downloading to a Printer

Your camera may offer you the capability of downloading your images directly to a printer. Of course, you'll need to be sure that your printer can communicate with your camera.

With some cameras and printers, when you choose to download directly to a printer you are foregoing the option of editing your images. You may be able to make a few minor adjustments, such as rotating the image, but you will not be able to make major changes to an image.

One printer that does allow you to manipulate your images before downloading directly from your camera is the Kodak PPM200. Using this printer, you can insert a memory card into a slot on it, then use its picture preview screen to view, crop and size your images before printing. You also have the option of printing your pictures with frames or without. The Kodak PPM200 works with CompactFlash and SmartMedia storage devices.

A printer that offers infrared technology, along with a built-in reader for SmartMedia and CompactFlash memory cards, is the HP Photosmart 1218. The colour printer allows you to download images directly from your digital camera, PC, Mac, laptop computer or other digital device. It also provides a USB and parallel port for users who don't have an IrDA-equipped camera.

There are certain circumstances that make downloading digital images directly to a printer the best alternative. For instance, a teacher may want to use her camera in the classroom to catch her students in action. If she can quickly print out the stored images, the children can take pictures home with them on the same day. If the need to print digital images quickly is your top priority, then you may want to consider choosing a camera that provides direct printer output.

CHAPTER 15

Image Compression and File Formats

Compression reduces the size of an image file by either reducing the number of colours in an image or by grouping together a series of pixels of a similar colour. Because a compressed file takes up less space, you can fit more image files on your internal flash memory chip, removable storage media or hard drive when they are compressed.

How Compression Works

The number of digital images that fit on a memory card varies according to the resolution of each image, as it is the resolution that determines the size of each image. For instance, a memory card that holds 16 low-resolution images might hold just a single high-resolution image.

Let's take a closer look at how this works. A typical compact camera may output images with resolutions of either 1,792 x 1,184 or 896 x 592, depending on how compressed the images are. The user chooses one of three image-quality settings to determine the compression ratio.

If you choose the 'best' resolution setting, your images will be 1,792 x 1,184, which is roughly 2.1MB. To determine the size of the image, multiply that number by three, because every pixel in a colour digital image utilizes three bytes of information (one byte for red, one byte for blue and one byte for green). The result is 6.3MB. This would lead us to believe that a 16MB memory card could only store two images from the digital camera source. In reality, it can hold as many as 30 images. So what is the secret to squeezing in the extra images? Compression.

Ideally, your camera will allow you to choose the amount of compression used on a particular image. You can then determine the setting you want to utilize based on the resolution you need for the image. If you need your digital images to be of the very highest quality, select a camera that has a no-compression or low-compression option.

Experiment with compression levels on your camera and in your image-editing software to see what best meets your individual needs. You may find that when you apply less compression, the quality remains quite high while still saving you time on downloads.

Lossy Versus Lossless Compression

There are two types of compression: lossy and lossless. With lossless compression, no bits of information are permanently lost. This type of compression works by rearranging redundant pixels, but does not delete any of them. For this reason, lossless compression preserves image quality, but it also results in smaller decreases in file size. Lossless file formats include TIFF, GIF and BMP.

With lossy compression, some bits of information are permanently eliminated. Lossy compression results in significantly smaller file sizes, but image resolution is also reduced. JPEG is one example of a lossy file format. Another, less used one, is FlashPix.

File Formats

The term 'file format' refers to a method of storing computer data. There are many different file formats, including proprietary ones used exclusively by a particular camera manufacturer or a particular software manufacturer. Some formats can be used only with Macintosh computers; others can be used only with PCs. The more popular formats are supported by most programs across both platforms. The following is an overview of popular file formats.

JPEG (JPG)

JPEG is the image compression method most widely utilized by digital cameras. JPEG stands for Joint Photographic Experts Group, the people who developed the original code. Because of its ability to reduce file size with a negligible degree of deterioration, JPEG has become the standard for saving and compressing digital images.

JPEG is a very efficient method of compression that preserves colours well. It accom-modates both 8-bit greyscale and 24-bit colour images. JPEG rearranges or deletes pixels to reduce the size of digital images. The resulting compressed images take up from 2 to 50 per cent of the space they would have used if they were left as uncompressed images.

As you can see, compressing files to JPEG results in great savings of space on memory cards and hard drives. However, since JPEG is a lossy compression scheme, each time that an image is compressed using JPEG, there is a corresponding decrease in resolution. Every time a photographer edits or resaves a JPEG file, the quality of the image deteriorates. Because of the pixel elimination that happens during JPEG compression, the decompressed image is not going to be identical to the original.

> In a nutshell, JPEG uses a lot of compression and JPEG images are good for using on a website or with e-mail, while TIFF uses much less compression and TIFF images are best for photos you want to print.

One great advantage of JPEG is that you can control the degree of compression. For instance, with some image-editing software programs, such as Adobe Photoshop, you can compress JPEG files in a variety of preset levels, ranging from maximum (highest compression) to low (lowest compression), thereby altering the resulting quality of the image. You can determine how you want to balance file size with image quality.

Using low-compression/higher-quality settings will give you bigger files but better images. Higher-quality images always look better, even at lower resolutions. And since you have more pixels to play with, they provide better results when used with an image-editing software program.

JPEG2000 (JP2)

The Joint Photographic Experts Group and others also developed a new image coding system using state-of-the-art compression techniques. It is called JPEG2000 and was has been available since 2001. JPEG2000 provides users of digital cameras with a more versatile JPEG file format that uses wavelet technology, which is a significant advancement in image compression.

With JPEG, compression is performed on 8 x 8 blocks of pixels. When you use the highest level of compression or enlarge a compressed image greatly, the blocks become visible to the human eye. Wavelet technology does not divide images into blocks the way JPEG does; it uses a continuous stream. Therefore, images in the JPEG2000 format suffer less degradation at a higher compression ratio, enabling them to take up less space but provide better resolution.

The JPEG2000 format based on wavelet technology provides users with certain advantages over the original JPEG standard. JPEG2000 offers the following:

- Comparable image quality with files that are 25–35 per cent smaller in size
- Improved image quality at the same file size
- Good image quality even at compression ratios as high as 80:1 and higher
- A single compressed file offers a variety of options, which vary depending on need. Options include image sizes ranging from thumbnail to full size; greyscale to full three-channel colour; and low-res images to those identical to the original.

TIFF (TIF)

TIFF (Tagged Image File Format) allows you to store the highest-quality uncompressed images. It is the most popular lossless compression format. The TIFF format supports 8-bit greyscale and 24-bit colour images. In addition, it accommodates 1-bit black and white, 8-bit colour and numerous other colour settings.

You should consider using TIFF if you plan to edit your images repeatedly, use them in a publishing software program, or if you want to produce high-contrast photos. TIFF is not a good choice for images that you will be using on websites or e-mailing, since it cannot shrink images to their smallest possible size, leaving you with the problem of having images that take a very long time to send and be received.

When manipulating digital images in an image-editing software program, save them as a TIFF file or the program's proprietary file format to preserve their quality. Once you have finished editing the image, save the image as a JPEG.

EXIF

EXIF stands for Exchangeable Image Format and is a variation of the JPEG format. It was developed by the Japanese Electronics Industry Development Association. Some digital cameras may store images as EXIF in order to record extra information with the file, such as the aperture, shutter speeds and other camera settings; picture-taking conditions; sounds recorded when the image was captured, and more. This extra information is known as metadata. Camera specifications sometimes note this type of format as JPEG (EXIF).

GIF

Another lossless compression format, GIF stands for Graphic Interchange Format. GIFs use a simple technique called LZW compression to reduce the file sizes of images by finding repeated patterns of pixels, but this compression never degrades the image quality.

GIF files can be saved with a maximum of 256 colours. This makes it a poor format for photographic images. Because this can sometimes be tight, GIFs will mix pixels of two different available colours to create a suggestion of another colour.

PNG

PNG (Portable Network Graphics) is a format invented specifically for the Internet. One version of the format, PNG-8, is similar to GIF. It can be saved with a maximum of 256 colours and supports 1-bit transparency. File sizes when saved in a capable image editor like FireWorks will be noticeably smaller than the GIF counterpart, as PNGs save their colour data more efficiently.

PNG-24 is another flavour of PNG, with 24-bit colour support, allowing ranges of colour akin to a high colour JPEG. PNG-24 is not a replacement format for JPEG, however, because it is a lossless compression format. This means that file sizes can be rather big against a comparable JPEG. Using PNG-8 in place of static GIFs will lower the file sizes of your images.

If your image has fewer than 256 colours, then there will be no degradation of quality when you choose to save it as a GIF or PNG file format. Since the format is not saving colour information for unused colours, the file size will be reduced. But if your image contains lots of subtle variation in colour, its quality will be greatly decreased.

GIF, JPEG and PNG are the formats most commonly used on the Internet. Most colour images and backgrounds on the Internet are GIF or PNG files, which accommodate 8-bit colour, giving you the option to have an image display up to 256 colours. This is far fewer than the 16 million colours recognized by JPEG and TIFF. However, you should note that the user chooses which colours GIF and PNG will use, and they can come from any of the 16 million available from the 24-bit colour library. An index lists the colours contained in the file. GIF and PNG are good file formats for line drawings, text and graphics.

EPS

EPS stands for Encapsulated PostScript. EPS files incorporate the PostScript language and the original file, so files saved in the EPS format are larger than the original. Adobe created PostScript as a means of communicating to a printer the size of the file, what fonts it uses and other details so that the printer can output an accurate document. This format is utilized primarily for top-end desktop publishing and graphics output. Because they are cumbersome, EPS files do not work well on the Internet.

PDF

An updated version of the EPS format, PDF (portable document format) also contains information that is helpful to the printer, including descriptions of font, size and colour. The PDF file is not really just one file; it is an entire document that can include images, colour and the like.

A PDF file easily accommodates a large document, making it an excellent method for transmitting data via the Internet, and PDF readers are readily available. Many software companies are distributing their software manuals as PDF files.

Native Formats

Many software programs save files to native (proprietary) formats, which are designed to support the program's special features. For instance, PhotoDeluxe uses the PDD format, and Photoshop uses the PSD (Photoshop document) format. Remember that if you want to use your image with a different program, you will need to save it to another format, such as JPEG or TIFF.

Platform-Specific Formats

There are some formats that are not particularly useful for digital photographers, but you should be aware that they exist. One is PICT, which is the native graphics format used by the Macintosh operating system and can only be read by Macintosh programs. Another is BMP, which is a standard bitmap file format designed by Microsoft to handle images in Windows programs. Neither format works particularly well with digital images. It is better to save your images as JPEGs or TIFFs.

Compression (Archive) Formats

If you have many large digital image files to manage, you may want to investigate zip files. These files are the most common type of archive format and are designed to help you distribute and store files. Zip files contain one or more other files, which are usually compressed first. You can easily and quickly group, transport and copy zip files.

There are other file formats that provide benefits similar to zip files. These include TAR, gzip, ARJ, LZH and CAB.

There are dozens of compression and archiving utilities available that will allow you to shrink images, making them easier to archive or use on the Internet. Below are summaries of a few long-established ones. Be aware that if you 'zip' your files and send them via e-mail, the receiver must have the necessary software to 'unzip' them.

WinZip

WinZip is a powerful yet easy to use compression utility. The program includes long file name support and tight integration with Windows systems, including 95, 98, NT, 2000, Me and XP. You can drag and drop to or from Windows Explorer, or zip and unzip within Explorer. Popular Internet file formats that it supports include ZIP, TAR, gzip, CAB, UUEncode, Xxencode, BinHex and MIME. ARJ, LZH and ARC files are supported via external programs. WinZip will help you access almost all the files you download from the Internet. WinZip has won numerous awards, including the Shareware Industry Award 2000 for Best Overall Utility, the People's Choice Award 2000 for Best Application, the Best Utility MVP Award from *PC Computing* (January 2000), and was voted Download of the Millennium on ZDNet. A free evaluation version of WinZip can be downloaded from *www.winzip.com*.

BitZipper

Another excellent archive utility is BitZipper from Bitberry Software. You can download a free trial version at *www.bitberry.com*. BitZipper is an easily used utility that offers full support for many file formats, including ZIP, CAB, BH, GZ, JAR, LHA, LZH and TAR. In addition, it offers partial support (view and extract) for ACE, ARC, ARJ, RAR, RGZ, UUE, XXE, Z and ZOO formats. BitZipper allows you to create, view and extract from ZIP files, apply password protection and read and add comments. With the BitZipper Batch Tool, you will be able to extract, convert, search and virus scan multiple archives in one operation. BitZipper supports Windows 9x, NT, 2000, Me and XP. BitZipper has been recognized by ZDNet, Winfiles.com, Yahoo! Internet Life, Yippee Shareware and others.

FilZip

FilZip is a free zip program that lets you zip and unzip compressed archives. It has features such as password protection, multiple-disk archive support, zip file comment support and self-extracting zips. It supports many archive formats, including ZIP, ACE, ARC, ARJ, CAB, GZ, LAH, JAR, RAR and TAR. With FilZip, you can create new zip files, edit existing zip files, unzip multiple archives in a single operation and view and extract individual files from within zip files. A free download is available at *www.filzip.com*.

StuffIt Deluxe

Macintosh users can utilize the StuffIt Deluxe program from Aladdin Systems to compress image files. The program helps you create and send e-mail attachments faster, back up more files as archives and squeeze more images onto Zip disks, CDs and other removable media. StuffIt Deluxe works with most file formats, including StuffIt, Zip, Bzip, BinHex, MacBinary, Uuencode, gzip, Tape Archive Format, ARC, Compact Pro, DiskDoubler, LHA, RAR, MIME, Z, AppleLink, Private File and more. Perhaps the most popular compression utility for the Mac, StuffIt Deluxe has been recognized by CNET, MacFixIt, Applelinks.com, and others. The program is available from Aladdin Systems at *www.allume.com*.

CHAPTER 16

Storing Your Digital Images

I f you take a lot of pictures, sooner or later you are going to want to create a storage system that allows you to easily access your images. The advent of the megapixel digital camera has resulted in the ability to capture higher-resolution images that provide greater detail. The downside? These images require much more storage space than earlier, low-resolution images.

Understanding Computer Memory

There are several different ways to approach storing your digital images. Storage options run from hard drives to CDs and DVDs to memory cards used in your digital camera. (You can find more on removable memory in Chapter 6.) With a little planning, you will be able to utilize one or more of the powerful and flexible computer-based storage and management tools available today.

Taking a look inside your computer will give you a better idea of how data is stored.

- Data stored temporarily in your computer is stored in RAM (random-access memory).
- There are two types of RAM: cache and system RAM.
- RAM is considered to be 'volatile' because it stores data and allows access to it as long as an electric current is maintained. Once the power is turned off, everything stored in RAM is lost.
- There are two types of cache: Level I is small and is located in the processor itself. It stores data that is needed quickly. Level II cache is larger and originally was an external memory, but increasingly it is being placed directly into the CPU core. Level II cache stores data that is needed less quickly.
- System RAM holds information that is critical to your applications and operating systems. As you add more applications to your computer, you will be using up more RAM.
- A PC should have at least 128MB of RAM in order to run Windows 98, ME, NT, 2000 or XP without difficulty.
- You'll know that your computer is low on RAM if you hear your hard drive spinning while you edit large files or switch between applications.

Saving Your Images

The first step towards storing your digital images is to choose how you will save them.

Choosing a File Format

As discussed in Chapter 15, a file format can be compressed or uncompressed. Uncompressed file formats take up more storage space but offer you the maximum amount of image-forming information. Compressed file formats sometimes delete information in order to reduce the file and conserve storage space.

Many digital imaging experts recommend initially saving your digital files as TIFF files. These act in the same way that negatives do in a 35mm system. By saving your images as TIFF files, you will preserve their image quality. Then you can make duplicate files and save them as compressed files, such as JPEG, to use for e-mailing, on websites, or for printing.

Storage Devices

There are two main types of storage technologies: magnetic and optical. Magnetic media include Zip and floppy disks and hard drives. Optical media include CD-ROM and DVD.

Magnetic media are inexpensive and quick and easy to use. But these media are not archival; the information contained on magnetic media will degrade over time. They are also more adversely affected by the environment than optical media are.

Optical media drives are more expensive, but they are designed to provide archival storage capabilities. In fact, Kodak's premium CDs are designed to last more than 80 years. Recently, however, some concerns have arisen about the viability of CDs as a long-term storage device. An article in the American *Wall Street Journal* reported that CDs could prove to have problems, saying, 'Disks have turned out to be surprisingly vulnerable to fingerprints, heat, even something called laser rot.'

The type of storage device you choose for your images will depend to some degree on how you plan to use them. Do you want to transport them to a digital lab to have prints made? Or are you hoping that your images will be around for as long as you will?

Magnetic Media

Most people are familiar with magnetic media. Below we look at the common types of magnetic media that photographers use for the storage of digital images.

Hard Drives

The hard drive is the internal memory of your computer, which acts as a filing cabinet where you store files. You can choose to store all of your files on your hard drive, or use removable media in addition to or in place of your hard drive. Even if you use your hard drive as your primary place of storage, you will want to back up your files in case your hard drive should ever fail.

Hard drives are not costly. To determine the size of the hard drive you will need, you'll have to consider your storage needs and habits. If you like to keep everything on your computer for quick access, you'll probably want to buy the biggest hard drive you can afford.

If you've filled up your computer's hard drive and want to purchase an external one to hold all your images, there is a bewildering range and variety available. At time of writing, the title of the world's smallest and therefore most portable external hard drive is held by the tiny Freecom FHD-XS, which, despite its pocket size, can hold up to 40GB (GigaBytes) of data. The same company makes a series of Classic models, which can hold up to 250GB and can be connected by FireWire and USB connections.

Other current top sellers in the external drive market include the Lacie D2, Maxtor OneTouch and 5000DV, Amazom EZ, VTEC USB2, Archos Qdisk and various models from Iomega and Western Digital. Check the websites listed in Chapter 4 for more detailed information and the latest developments in specifications.

Super Floppies/Zip Drives

Super floppies are just a bit bigger than standard floppy disks, but they hold considerably more data. Iomega makes the Zip drive, a popular super floppy available in 100MB and 250MB versions. The Iomega Zip supports many operating systems and interfaces, including Microsoft Windows 95,

98, NT, 3.x, Me and XP, and Macintosh 8, 9 and X systems. Zip drives are available as both external and internal drives. Using Zip disks is like using preformatted floppy disks, as they are enclosed and almost impossible to scratch.

Iomega also makes the Jaz, another external drive. The Jaz is fast, with transfer rates of up to 16MB per second. Using one 2GB Jaz disk, you can transport files, store 2,000 photos (640 x 480 pixels) or 20–40 minutes of compressed video, or run individual applications.

Floppy Disks

Just about everyone is familiar with the ubiquitous, if now old-fashioned, floppy disk. Floppy disks provided an easy method of transporting files when virtually all computers had floppy disk drives. Although inexpensive and readily available, they provided limited storage space and images needed to be low-resolution or highly compressed if you were to store them on a floppy disk.

Early digital cameras, such as the Sony Mavica range, used floppy disks, but the disks have become virtually superseded. You may be able to pick up very inexpensive cameras and computers that still use this technology, but the lack of speed and storage will be very noticeable.

Optical Media

There are several types of optical media that digital photographers can utilize. Below we'll examine what benefits they provide for the digital photographer.

CD-R and CD-RW

One storage solution is to use CDs with a CD-Recordable (CD-R) or CD-Rewritable (CD-RW) drive. CDs (and other removable media) will protect you against a faulty drive and provide you with an ideal means of backing up your hard drive. Using CDs, you can easily expand your storage system. As your needs increase, you simply purchase more CDs. They provide lots of storage space, since one CD-R can hold up to 650MB of images. And they are economical, since each CD-R costs very little.

Another important benefit of CDs is that their technology is likely to be around for a long time.

Most computers come with a CD-ROM drive, which lets you read CDs. In order to write files to CDs, you will need to purchase a writable CD drive, which allows you to both write and read data.

There are two different types of writable CDs. CD-R disks allow you to record on them only once, but it is impossible to overwrite your original file, which can be an advantage. A CD-RW disk can be used again, but you must erase all data before recording new data onto it. Keep in mind that if you decide to use a rewritable CD drive, you'll need special software to write to ('burn') CD-RW disks.

An easy way to get your images written to a CD is to get an image-processing service to do it for you. Many services will give you a hard copy of thumbnails showing each of your images, along with software that lets you view your images. If you want to have your images printed, this service can be completed at the same time.

Take these steps to ensure that your CDs last for a long time:

· Buy a high-end CD, not a bargain brand that may be made with inferior coatings.
· Keep your CDs in their jewel cases. If you do use plastic sleeves for storage, be sure they contain no PVC.
· Never leave writable CDs in direct sunlight.
· Do not flex a CD.
· If you clean your CD, use products made for cleaning photo lenses.
· Only use CD pens to write on a CD, and don't apply adhesive labels. If you've already labelled your CDs, do not try to take off the labels.
· Try to keep your CDs at low humidity and at temperatures below 25°C (77°F).

DVDs

The DVD (digital versatile disk) is a high-capacity optical medium that has already greatly replaced VHS tapes for videos, and is likely to replace CD-ROM and laserdiscs as well. However, before that can happen, DVD standards have still to be developed and utilized throughout the industry.

A DVD is a disk equivalent in size to a CD. Like a CD, it stores data in small spiral indentations and is read by a laser beam. The difference between the CD and DVD is that a DVD is read by a laser beam of a shorter wavelength than the CD so a DVD can utilize smaller indentations and, therefore, provide increased storage capacity. Today's DVD can store up to 25GB of data on a 125mm (5in) disk.

A DVD-ROM is a read-only DVD. It utilizes two layers. The outer layers can hold 4.7GB, while the underlying layer can hold 3.8GB. A two-sided disk accommodates 25GB of storage space. A DVD-R is a writable DVD that can be written to just once, similar to a CD-R. DVD-RAM is a readable and writable disk, which holds either 3.6GB or 4.7GB of files. A special cartridge holds the disks, which are extremely sensitive to contaminants. Because of the cartridge, a DVD-RAM cannot be utilized with a standard DVD player.

What's in a Name?

We all know what software is... well, sort of. Software is a general term used for programs that are designed to perform specific tasks within a computer. But there are different classes of software you should know about. Here's an overview:

- *Firmware:* Firmware is not really software; it is data-programmed into the circuitry of some hardware components of your computer. Firmware contains programming code that communicates to the equipment how it should operate. On the other hand, software is stored in read/write memory and can be easily altered.
- *Freeware:* Freeware is software that is available for download and unlimited use and is totally free to the user. Freeware includes utilities, desktop pictures and fonts.
- *Postcardware:* The developer of postcardware allows you to use the software without paying a fee but requests that you send him or her a postcard so she or he can get feedback and judge the popularity of the product.

- *Shareware:* Shareware refers to an application or utility that you can try out for free. Sometimes it is a fully featured product, and at other times it lacks some of the features of the commercial version. If you like it and want to continue to use it, you'll have to register the software and pay a small fee to the program's author.
- *Vaporware:* Vaporware is software that is announced a long time before it is ready for sale. Sometimes problems arise during development, and it never reaches the marketplace at all.

CHAPTER 17

Scanners

A scanner 'digitizes' photographs, allowing you to make changes and print out your photos or post them online. Today, historians use scanners to rescue old negatives and prints, botanists scan seeds and pressed flowers, and zoologists scan fish and insects to record scale and colour patterns. This chapter examines the uses of scanners in digital photography and what to look for when purchasing such a device.

What Is a Scanner and Why Do I Need One?

A scanner is a device that takes a picture of a page. In more technical terms, a scanner is an array of photosensitive silicon cells that measure the light reflected off – or transmitted through – the original. These measurements are then mapped onto levels (for example, 256 levels per primary colour for a 24-bit scanner) by an analogue-to-digital converter and stored as binary digits that you can view and manipulate with your computer. Basically, what the scanner is doing is turning the components of a slide, negative or print into digital data. Now that you know what a scanner is, the question remains: do you really need one?

That's a good question. About 25 years ago, there weren't too many people who could afford to have a scanner hooked up to their computer. Even 12 or so years ago, scanners had come down in price substantially, but they still cost as much as most computers. Today, flatbed scanners are affordable and are becoming a standard peripheral for many computer users. Although you don't have to have one, you'll find that a scanner will allow you to do a lot of wonderful things at an affordable price.

What kinds of things can scanners do? As mentioned above, scanners allow you to take existing photographs and digitize them; once digitized, the photographs can be permanently archived on a disk. Scanners offer substantially higher resolution than digital cameras, so you can create much higher image quality and enlarge pictures that might otherwise look grainy. And scanners allow you to import photographs into your computer and edit them using special image-editing software. (See Chapter 21 for more details on image-editing software.)

You can have fun scanning three-dimensional objects with your scanner. Because your scanner will place a slight shadow on one side of the object, you'll want to do a little experimenting with position. Scan the object, and if you don't like the effect you've achieved, reposition it on the glass platen and try again.

If you have a home office, scanners can also perform some additional functions. A scanner can act as a colour copier: just insert the original in the scanner, press the function button, and the copy can be printed on a colour printer. If your computer has a built-in modem, you can scan documents, newspaper clippings or layouts and send them to any fax machine in the world. You can also 'photograph' three-dimensional objects on a scanner and print or store the images.

Flatbed Scanners

If you are new to the world of digital photography, the chances are that you will probably want to purchase a flatbed scanner, the most popular model of desktop scanner. A flatbed scanner takes its name from the flat glass platen (or bed) where you place the object to be scanned. It is very versatile and can be used to scan flat materials such as photographs and printed pages.

There are three basic levels of flatbed scanners you can buy. The least expensive have a scanning area of 215 x 280mm ($8^1/_2$ x 11in) and cost under £60. They generally feature a horizontal resolution of 300dpi and 30- or 36-bit colour depth; although the bulk of the products available use charge-coupled device (CCD) sensors, the smallest and lightest flatbed units typically use a CMOS image sensor (CIS). Most scanners in this price range come with very little software.

Midlevel scanners feature a 280 x 430mm (11 x 17in) scanning area, and their cost ranges from £60 to about £150. Optical resolution on these models ranges from 400 to 600dpi and colour depth is 30 to 36 bits. These scanners usually come with image-editing and optical character recognition (OCR) software.

Higher-level flatbed scanners cost upwards of £150. These scanners feature a minimum 600dpi optical horizontal resolution, 30- or 36-bit colour, and high-quality bundled software such as Adobe Photoshop.

'Dots per inch' or dpi refers to the resolution of an image. This number tells you how much information is contained in a linear inch of an image. In general, the higher the resolution, the higher the quality of the image.

You want to purchase a scanner with an optical scanning resolution of at least 600dpi so that you can scan detailed images and line art from photographs or other printed originals.

Film Scanners

A transparency or film scanner allows you to scan everything from a 35mm slide to a 4 × 5in transparency. These scanners are more expensive than flatbed scanners, but they are excellent for people who want to scan a lot of transparencies because they are the only scanner that will produce quality transparency scans. However, if you only occasionally scan transparencies, a flatbed scanner with a transparency adapter is sufficient.

Film scanners generally feature an optical resolution of 1,200dpi or higher. In fact, most affordable transparency scanners scan images at 2,700dpi. That's because the higher resolution is needed to compensate for the small size of the item being scanned.

For film scanners, a more important measure is optical density (OD). OD measures the breadth of the tonal range – or brightness values – that a scanner can capture. Slides, film, negatives and transparencies have a broader tonal range than printed photographs. Because OD is directly related to bit depth, you want a scanner with a bit depth of 30 or higher. Although there is no direct correlation, a 36-bit scanner generally has a higher OD than a 24-bit scanner, provided all other things are equal.

The Acer ScanWit 2720 Film Scanner removes dust and scratches from images while you are scanning them. Using Applied Science Fiction's Digital ICE technology, this scanner also features 2,700dpi optical resolution and a dynamic range of 3.2. It can be bought for under £250, making it one of the cheapest quality film scanners on the market.

The Polaroid SprintScan 4000 is a 35mm film scanner that is both Windows and Macintosh compatible. It features 4,000 × 4,000dpi optical resolution, 3.4 density range, and 36-bit colour. Its high resolution allows users to work with smaller portions of an image and still maintain recognizable detail. It features the current shortest scan time for all scanners, of less than one minute per slide, and has a SCSI-2 fast interface.

The Nikon LS-400 Film Scanner delivers 130MB, 48-bit colour scans and has a dynamic range of 4.2. This scanner also features Applied Science Fiction's Digital ICE scratch and dust removal technology, as well as Digital ROC and digital GEM to help restore faded colours and make scans less grainy. An auto slide feeder handles up to 50 slides and incorporates a series of adapters for slide mounts. Nikon Scan 3 and Altamira Genuine Fractals 2.0 software come bundled with this scanner.

Combination Scanners

As you might have guessed, combination or multiformat scanners scan film and slides as well as flat printed materials. Until fairly recently, combination scanners did not do a good job scanning film and slides, but now there are a few combination scanners on the market that will allow you to produce good film and slide scans, as well as high-quality scans from the flatbed part of the scanner.

Although you might expect to pay quite a bit more for combination scanners because of their dual purpose, prices are tumbling all the time as the technology involved becomes more sophisticated and less expensive to produce. Shop around for a good deal.

The CanoScan D660U is a flatbed scanner with a built-in 35mm film adapter in the lid for scanning negatives and slides on the flatbed glass. It doesn't offer the resolution or the sharpness that you'll find with a dedicated film scanner, but it costs a lot less. It's a great choice for scanning images for use on the Internet or for e-mailing images to friends. It features a 600 × 1,200dpi CCD with 42-bit colour, and it recognizes more than a trillion colours. It can also handle 215 × 280mm (8$^{1}/_{2}$ × 11in) prints. The CanoScan D660U uses USB to connect with both Mac and Windows systems.

Drum Scanners

A professional wouldn't use anything but a drum scanner for producing colour separations. While other scanners use CCD technology (see Chapter 5), drum scanners use Photo Multiplier Tube (PMT) technology for greater colour accuracy. PMT detects light and splits it into three beams, passes it through red, green and blue filters, then converts the light into an electrical signal. Drum scanners also offer features that you won't see on ordinary desktop scanners, such as direct conversion to CMYK (see below), batch scanning, auto sharpening and huge image areas.

The biggest difference between drum scanners and other models is their speed: since the process of converting an image to CMYK is automatic, drum scanners can produce considerably more scans per hour than desktop models. The disadvantage of drum scanners is that some have price tags that run into the four-figure range. Although drum scanners are too expensive for most people, some professional printers will scan photographs using a drum scanner on a per-project basis.

Images are created on professional printing presses and many consumer printers using four colours of ink: cyan, magenta, yellow and black (CMYK) – the K is used for black so as not to be confused with blue. The black is necessary so that the black portions of an image come out black and not a shade of grey.

You should be aware that some inkjet printers only use three colours: cyan, magenta and yellow. However, colour can be severely compromised on these printers, and you won't get the same rich blacks that you get on a four-colour printer.

Handheld Scanners

Handheld scanners cost about a third to a quarter of the price of flatbed scanners, and they are very portable – you can plug them directly into a computer's printer port, so they can be easily shared by different workstations. Many people like to use them with their laptop computers.

Handheld scanners do have some disadvantages compared with flatbed scanners: they are less accurate and they have weaker light sources, so they sometimes produce uneven scans. They are also dependent on the steadiness of your hand or the surface you are standing on. (Many hand scanners offer an alignment template to overcome this and help you with more accurate scanning.)

There are some high-end hand scanners that offer 400dpi resolution and 24-bit colour, which allows you to achieve high-quality results. However, because the focus is on portability, their scan head is only 100 x 125mm (4 x 5in), which means that you have to make multiple passes to scan any images that are larger than 100 x 125mm (4 x 5in). What you'll have to do with a larger image is to stitch the parts of it together using software – this can be very tedious and time-consuming. Despite their disadvantages, handheld scanners are very popular because they are so portable and can produce quick and easy low-cost scans.

Small-Footprint Scanners

You can now find quite a few small-footprint scanners for under £150. Some of them take advantage of CMOS image sensor (CIS) technology, which allows the manufacturer to do away with the complex systems of lenses and mirrors required by a CCD-based model. Although CIS scan quality isn't yet up to that of CCDs, these scanners are smaller, lighter and more durable than their CCD-based counterparts, which make them ideal for taking on the road or fitting into cramped spaces such as spare rooms.

The UMAX Astra 3400 is an excellent low-priced scanner that can be used with both Windows and Macintosh computers. It features 600 x 1,200dpi optical resolution, 9,600 x 9,600dpi interpolated resolution and 42-bit colour. The maximum scan size is 215 x 298mm ($8^1/2$ x $11^3/4$in), and it comes with a transparency adapter that allows for 100 x 125mm (4 x 5in) scanning. It comes with SCSI-2 and USB interfaces.

Are More Bits Necessarily Better?

An important feature of scanners is their bit depth. Keep in mind that when it comes to bits, more is better. Bit depth doesn't refer to the actual number of colours the scanner can capture, but rather the number of levels it can enumerate – in other words, just because a scanner has the capacity to assign one of 16.8 million values to a colour (24-bit) doesn't mean that the sensor can distinguish between two close shades of grey or blue. That's why more bits will generally give you better image reproduction, even though your printer can't print and your screen can't display more than 16.8 million colours.

The minimum colour depth you should consider for scanning photos and documents is 24 bits (8 bits per colour or grey shade). Even the best 24-bit scanners suffer from noise, which usually results in a maximum of 6 usable bits per colour, rather than 8 bits. That's only about 262,144 colours, which falls short of the dynamic range of a typical photograph. In addition, those bits will be clustered around the midtones of the image, which means you'll lose detail in shadows and highlights. The images should be adequate for printouts on older, lower-quality printers, as well as Internet graphics and document management tasks.

If you're scanning slides, negatives or transparencies, which have a broader tonal range than printed photographs, 30 bits is the absolute minimum you should consider.

Be careful not to confuse common printing rules of thumb with scanner specifications. For instance, just because your high-end inkjet printer can only reproduce 24 bits of colour data , that doesn't mean you won't get better print output from a 36-bit scan than you would from a 24-bit scan. In theory, a higher bit depth should always be better than a lower. Unfortunately, some flatbed scanner vendors are not clear or consistent when they define bit depth. For instance, some manufacturers use a 24-bit CCD and combine it with a 10-bit rather than a standard 8-bit ADC to stretch the output range of the colours into the shadows and highlights. This doesn't add any information, but it can potentially make the existing image data look a little better. So, in this case, a very good 24-bit scanner can still give you better images than a mediocre 30-bit one.

Which Scanner Is Right for You?

The good news is that there are many affordable scanners on the market today. The bad news is that it can be confusing to determine which one is right for you. Here are a few points that might help you to clarify which model is best for you.

Price

How much do you want to spend on your scanner? As we mentioned earlier, you can pay thousands of pounds for a top-quality scanner, but the ones that you will be looking at probably range in price from under £50 to £400 or so.

Purpose

What do you want to scan? Flat things such as magazine clippings, photographs or pages of books? Slides or negatives? A combination of both (possibly the most likely in time)? The answer to this question will determine what type of scanner you should purchase.

Resolution, Colour Depth and Density Range

These three factors will determine the quality of your scanned images. Optical resolution determines how sharp your image will be; this, in turn, determines how large your image can become, because low-resolution images become grainy when they are enlarged. A good rule of thumb is to choose a scanner with a minimum of 600dpi. Make sure that you are looking at the optical resolution rating and not the interpolated dpi rating, which is the resolution that can be achieved with the help of software.

Although an optical resolution of 600dpi is sufficient for most people, you will want to invest in a scanner that offers higher optical resolution if you intend to produce a lot of large images. When comparing resolution specs, you need to watch for two measures. The optical resolution of the scanner's CCD (a row of sensors that moves vertically down the scan bed) determines how much real information the scanner captures. In contrast, the maximum interpolated resolution is what the scanner can achieve by using various optical enhancements and firmware algorithms to 'fill in the gaps' between actual pixels. If you need more data – to pick up finer details in line art, complex edges in images or fine print, for example – then you need to go for higher optical resolution. If you simply want more dots – to scale the size up so it will print at the appropriate size – you can settle for a high interpolated resolution.

For most tasks, a scanner with an optical resolution of 300dpi should be sufficient. This is also true for low-res proofs and placing the image on a printed page, capturing images and putting them on a webpage, and printing text. Choosing a scanner with a minimum dpi of 600 will allow you to scan detailed images and line art from photos or other printed originals.

Be careful not to confuse specifications for scanners and printers – they are not the same. (If it were that simple, you wouldn't need this book.) Even though your printer may require no more than 150dpi, you would rarely want to scan an image at that resolution.

One of the reasons you need to scan at a higher resolution than you print is that editing the photo in your computer causes the image to degrade. Whenever possible, scan the image at a higher resolution than is necessary, and your results will be better.

If you can afford a high-resolution scanner, it is a good investment. Even when they are scanning images at a lower resolution, higher-resolution scanners always print images that are sharper and have more detail. So a 150dpi image scanned on a 600dpi scanner is always going to have more detail than a 150dpi image scanned on a 300dpi scanner.

If bigger is better when it comes to resolution, the same must be true for colour depth, right? Sorry, no. Colour depth is an important factor in image quality, but things are not so clear-cut in this area. For example, some 24-bit scanners produce lower-quality scans than some inexpensive 6-bit scanners. So while colour depth is something to keep in mind when shopping for a scanner, it's not as important or as reliable a measure as optical resolution or density range.

Optical density (OD) range is defined as a measurement of the breadth of the tonal range – or brightness value – that a scanner can capture. This is directly related to optical resolution. Density range is the most important value for film scanners and professional scanners, but many consumer-level scanners do not offer density value ratings. For this reason, OD is the best way to differentiate between a good graphics scanner and a consumer-level device; if the scanner lists its OD rating, it's probably a higher-quality model. The average flatbed scanner provides an OD of between 2.8 and 3.0, which is fine for scanning most photographs. Slides and transparencies require at least 3.2 OD for a decent scan, and negatives require 3.4 OD or more.

CIS Versus CCD

For a long time, the only desktop scanners available were CCD-based scanners. Then a less expensive competitor – CIS (which stands for both contact image sensor and CMOS image sensor) – came along. Both are made of silicon, and both use on-chip filters to separate light into red, green and blue. A CCD-based scanner requires an analogue-to-digital converter (ADC) to translate the sensor data into binary information, while a CIS sensor has built-in logic to perform this task.

The advantage of owning a CIS-based scanner is that it requires fewer components than a CCD-based scanner, which means that it takes up less space, uses less power and costs less to manufacture. But there is another factor: the on-chip ADC logic takes up space that might otherwise be devoted to light sensing, so current CIS sensors tend to have a smaller dynamic range than CCDs. In addition, because CIS scanners are relatively new, manufacturers don't have as much experience at fine-tuning the noise reduction and filtering algorithms as they do for CCD scanners (although the catch-up rate is increasing here).

Scan Speed

Scan speed means just what you think it does – the amount of time that it takes to scan a single page at a specific resolution. Depending on whether you will be scanning a lot of images, and especially a lot of large images, speed may or may not be important to you. Scan speeds are also affected by your computer interface and, to a lesser extent, by scanning software.

Scanner Interface

Interface refers to the connection between your scanner and your computer. A SCSI interface is generally fastest, followed by USB and then parallel interfaces. If you plan to use your scanner with several personal computers, USB might be your best choice, because USB interfaces are easier to install than SCSI interfaces. (See Chapter 14 for more on interfaces.)

Many low-cost scanners operate via a parallel connection with a pass-through connector for a printer, primarily because this is an inexpensive implementation for the manufacturer, and because every PC has a parallel port. On the downside, however, parallel scanners can be slow, and external parallel-based Zip drives can't use the pass-through connector. USB-compliant devices, the logical successor to parallels' market position, have made great inroads as these days nearly all systems are fitted with USB ports. If you've got the choice, opt for USB over a parallel connection for greater reliability and configuration flexibility.

In general, any scanner with an optical resolution of more than 600dpi and a colour depth of 36 bits or more will come with a SCSI connector, which can handle high-bandwidth applications such as graphics designed for print and high-volume document management.

If you find a low-priced scanner with less impressive specs that has a SCSI interface, the chances are that it's an old model. You are better off choosing a scanner that connects via parallel or USB. (Note that SCSI scanners usually include their own controller cards, but these adapters aren't good choices for other devices.)

Scanner Software

The software that you use with your scanner can make a big difference in image quality and the speed with which you can scan. With some software, you can scan an image with a single click of a button, while other software packages require a two-step process: you must look at a preview of the image after it is scanned, and then wait again while the final image is made. Some software allows you to optimize the image, whereas other packages offer you little control. Chapter 21 looks at some popular image-editing software.

When you scan a page, you end up with a file that consists of a mass of dots. To turn this file into text you can edit, you have to run it through optical character recognition (OCR) software to 'translate' it – all but the oldest scanners come bundled with limited editions of OCR packages.

Image-editing software lets you manipulate the tones and colours of an image to make it display or print better. It also gives you filters to apply special effects.

Extras

Some scanners offer special features that you might find useful for certain situations – for example, some Nikon scanners enable batch scans and come with software that automatically removes dust and scratches. Some scanners come with transparency adapters, and some have automatic document feeders. Others come with a bundle of software that you might find attractive.

A transparency adapter is sometimes packaged as a scanner extra, but in most cases you'll have to purchase one separately. To scan negatives, slides and transparencies, you need to place the original between the light source and the sensor array so that the light passes through them before hitting the sensor. However, typical flatbed scanners place the light source and sensor array on the same side, to catch the light as it reflects off the original. You need a transparency adapter (also called TPA or TPU) – a backlight that replaces the scanner cover – to handle these kinds of originals. Not all scanners support a TPA, so it's a good move to ask before you buy if you think you may need one.

An automatic document feeder (ADF) is a good investment if you are going to be doing volume scanning.

There are a great many factors you'll want to take into consideration when you decide which scanner to purchase. You can look at the different brands and models at a national retail chain (Jessops, Dixons, PC World), at a specialist computer store, or by visiting the manufacturers' websites listed in Appendix B. Many retailers' websites provide information about scanners and allow you to search by manufacturer, merchant, computer type, interface and price, as well as featuring product reviews by users.

Handy Tools

After you purchase your scanner, you'll need to keep a few basic tools on hand. These include a can of compressed air, glass cleaner, a lens brush, black paper, a spare scanner bulb, screwdrivers and black paper masks for 6mm ($1/4$in) and 100 x 125mm (4 x 5in) transparencies and negatives. You can get rid of dirt and dust spots on photographs after you scan them into your computer, but it's much easier to keep your photos and scanner as clean as possible. In other words, the cleaner you keep your scanner, the less work you'll have later.

Where Do Your Scans Go?

Once you scan your images, you'll have to decide what to do with them. The format you use to save your image will depend on how you want to use it. Some popular image file formats include:

· Native tongue format
· GIF (Graphics Interchange Format)
· JPEG (Joint Photographic Experts Group)
· TIFF (Tagged Image File Format).

The first format is the native tongue format – for example, Adobe Photoshop saves images in Photoshop format. The other three formats are shared formats, which can be read by a number of applications. Each of these has a different purpose. GIF and JPEG formats are best for Internet images – they have the right resolution for webpages or e-mail, and they don't use up a lot of disk space; JPEG is great for photographs, and GIF is best for artwork and detailed images. TIFF format is best for sharing images with other applications, as even word processing or spreadsheet programs can understand what a TIFF file is. The downside to TIFF files is that they are huge and not particularly suited to the Internet. For more on file formats, see Chapter 15.

Tips for Good Scanning

Here are a few techniques that will help you to create better images with your scanner.

- *Practise, practise, practise!* Don't be discouraged if your initial scans aren't great. Scanning is an art on its own, and the more you practise with different images using your particular scanner and computer, the better you'll become at it.
- *Choose your best photos.* Although there are a lot of things you can do to correct an image in your computer, it is always better to pay attention to things like proper exposure when you are taking your pictures. It's also a good idea to keep your scanner as clean as possible so you don't have to remove spots or marks in your computer.
- *Pay attention to image placement.* With a little practice, you'll learn how to correctly place images on your scanner. Rotating your image using software degrades it, so learning to place things properly on your scanner from the start is important.
- *Set your resolution.* Choosing the correct resolution is challenging, and not all scanner drivers do it the same way. A good rule of thumb is to always go slightly higher in dpi than you may need. However, going too large results in huge files that take up a lot of memory and require more computer time to work with. Depending on your scanner, you will be looking at one of the following measurements when you are setting your resolution for scanning:
    - Output resolution: if your scanner driver uses output resolution as a measurement, set it to 240 to 300dpi and the final print size to the largest print you are likely to make – for example, your choice might be an 200 x 255mm (8 x 10in) print at 300dpi.
    - File size: choose a 5MB file for an excellent 100 x 150 mm (4 x 6in) print, 10MB for 125 x 178mm (5 x 7in), and 20MB for 200 x 255mm (8 x 10in).
    - Input resolution: if your scanner driver uses input resolution, you'll have to do some calculating – you might choose 300dpi as your output resolution and 200 x 255mm (8 x 10in) as your final print size. You can then multiply 8 x 300 to get an input resolution of 2,400dpi.

CHAPTER 18

Printers

While you may enjoy viewing your digital images on a computer monitor, at some point you'll want to see a hard copy, so you need to purchase a printer that can supply you with good quality prints of your images. Conventional pictures printed in a darkroom are called photographs, but prints of digitized photos are generally known as 'photorealistic' prints. As printers become better, the difference between the two is lessening, but the difference in colour between photographs and photorealistic prints is substantial.

The Printing Process

Photographs are continuous-tone prints that contain an infinite variation of tones, colours and hues. If you looked through a loupe (a small magnifying glass used to examine photographs) to examine a photograph, you wouldn't see any white space or dot patterns. Digital prints, on the other hand, can generate 24-bit colour, which means that they can reproduce 16.7 million colours. Although that sounds like a lot, it really isn't that many when you realize the billions of colour variations that the human eye can distinguish. And because of the way digital printers represent colour, most can only print a fraction of these 16 million colours. Printers also do not print colour continuously; instead, they lay colour on a print dot by dot – thousands of dots are placed on a page per second, but they are still individual dots. If the resolution of the print is too low or the printer can't generate images with tight dot patterns, the quality of the print will suffer.

Colour printers for home or small business use can be purchased for under £100. Printers in the middle of the range offer high print quality, while if you spend more, you'll gain faster output speed and additional features, such as the ability to print directly from your camera's memory card or dual paper trays. The following represent the different types of printers and the advantages and disadvantages of each.

Inkjet Printers

Inkjet printers work by forcing little drops of ink through nozzles onto the paper. Consumer inkjet printers have been around for many years, but most initially produced images of poor quality. Today's inkjet printers produce excellent photorealistic prints. They are designed for home or small business use, and prices again start at under £100. With inkjet printers, you can output pictures on plain paper or thicker, glossy photographic-type paper stock. If you use the latter, the inkjet printer will pump out more ink onto it than it will on a plain piece of paper, so your images will be sharper. The best inkjet printers are those that use more than the standard CMYK colours. Inkjet printers that use a five-colour cartridge with cyan, magenta, yellow, light cyan and light magenta can emulate subtleties of skin tones. The colour inkjet printer has become the standard output device for many digital photographers.

What are the disadvantages of inkjet printers? Images can sometimes look a little fuzzy because ink droplets have a tendency to spread out when they hit the paper. This phenomenon, where colours bleed into each other, is known as dot gain, but in response to this problem, some printer manufacturers are now including dot gain compensation controls on their inkjet printers. The wet ink that is forced onto the paper can also cause paper to warp slightly, and prints can smear if you don't allow them to dry properly. You can lessen these problems by only using specially coated inkjet paper in your printer. The newer models of inkjet printers feature less colour bleeding and paper warping; however, the image on an inkjet print will still be destroyed if it gets wet.

At a price of under £100, the Canon S450 Bubble Jet Printer is one of the least expensive quality colour inkjet printers you can buy. It features 1,440 × 720dpi resolution, and it has a colour ink cartridge that is composed of three separate and replaceable cyan, magenta and yellow ink tanks – the advantage to this system is that if one colour becomes depleted, this is the only one that needs to be replaced. The Canon S450 comes with both USB and parallel ports and can be used with Windows 95/98, NT4, 2000, Me and XP, as well as with any Macintosh with OS 8.1 or higher. This printer comes bundled with a lot of utility software, including Canon Photo, OfficeReady CC, CreataCard, PrintMasterSE and TextBridge Pro.

Dye Sublimation Printers

For many years, dye sublimation printers have been heralded as the top-of-the range output device for digital printing. Dye subs (for short) transfer images to paper using a plastic film or ribbon coated with colour dyes. During the printing process, heating elements move across the film, causing the dye to fuse to the paper. The printers work by fusing dye onto the specially manufactured transfer paper, making a separate pass through the printer for each colour.

The advantages of dye sub printers are that they produce a high-quality, continuous-tone image with little or no evidence of pixelization. Dye sublimation printers are either three-colour (cyan, magenta and yellow), or four-colour (cyan, magenta, yellow and black).

Some printer manufacturers (such as Alps Electric) have developed printers that enable you to print in either dye sub mode or another 'everyday' print mode.

Despite their advantages, there are several disadvantages to dye sub printers. First, the ones that are available for the consumer market only produce snapshot-sized prints, so you can't use them to output letters, invoices and other full-page text documents. Second, the cost of consumables, particularly of the dye ribbon, is relatively high. Print paper for dye sub printers is also more expensive than photographic paper of equivalent size. Finally, questions have arisen about the stability of the dyes used over time, especially when prints come in contact with certain protective sleeves.

Thermo-Autochrome Printers

A handful of printers use thermal wax to heat pigment-carrying wax from a print ribbon. They are faster than dye sublimation printers because they use sticks of wax or ribbons of dye rather than ink cartridges. The technique is similar to that seen on fax machines that print on thermal paper. The two major disadvantages of thermo-autochrome or thermal wax printers are that they reproduce colour using a halftoning process, and that they can only use specially manufactured paper.

Solid Inkjet Printers

Solid inkjet printers use sticks of crayon-like ink that are heated and dropped onto the paper. These printers were the first on the market that had the ability to print on many different types of paper. The fact that many different types of paper can be used in these printers is still one of their major advantages. However, the main disadvantage of solid inkjet printers is that they are not as photorealistic as standard inkjets and they do not print text detail well.

Colour Laser Printers

Colour laser printers use a technology similar to photocopiers; a laser beam produces electrical charges on a drum inside the printer. The drum then rolls ink onto the paper and heat is applied, which permanently affixes the toner to the page. Laser printers can also be more expensive than most printers – however, although the upfront costs may be higher, money can be saved in the long run on consumables such as toner, ink and paper. These printers are best for networked groups of people who need high-speed quality output.

The Epson Stylus Photo 870 is a photo-quality 215 x 280mm (8$^1/_2$ x 11in) format printer. It features a resolution of 1,440 x 720dpi, and has a six-colour ink system and a USB interface, with drivers for Mac OS 8.5 or later, Windows 98, 2000, Office and XP. Adobe PhotoDeluxe image-editing software and Sierra Imaging Image Expert, a general-purpose program for viewing, organizing, editing and printing images, are bundled with the printer, which can be purchased for under £85.

The Canon BJC-50 is a battery-powered, compact, bubble-jet photorealistic colour printer that weighs only 900g (2.1lb). It comes with a little case and is great to use if you're travelling with your camera and laptop computer.

Making Your Choice

After you have reviewed all the options, the final decision about which printer to buy will be based on your own personal needs and preferences. Do you want a printer that you can use directly with your camera, or do you plan on manipulating most of your photos on your computer? Is text quality important, or are you mainly concerned with photographic quality? Is speed important? How important is price? The answers to these questions will determine what printer is the best choice for you.

Types of Printing

Host-Based Printing

All the computation that turns pixels into prints is actually done inside your computer, not in your printer. With a host-based printer, your computer is tied up while you're printing, so you won't be able to do anything else while you print. Other host-based printers allow you to perform additional tasks, but your computer runs much more slowly. You can generally save money by purchasing a host-based printer.

Computer-Free Printing

Some printers allow you to print images directly from your digital camera's memory card or other storage device. Other printers provide you with the option of cabling your camera to your printer for direct image download. Digital print order format (DPOF) allows you to select the images that you want to print through your camera's user interface. The camera records your instructions and passes them onto the printer, and you can transfer images between the two devices. The downside of this technology is that you can't edit images on your computer.

The Kodak Personal Picture Maker 200 from Lexmark is a computerless printer. It features a 45mm ($1^3/4$in) LCD monitor, and CompactFlash and Secure Digital are included. Using the Picture Preview Screen, images can be edited with features such as rotate, crop, change brightness and auto-enhance, to name a few. The Kodak Personal Picture Maker 200 can print on several paper sizes, including 215 x 280mm ($8^1/2$ x 11in) and postcards. The printer retails for about £250.

Postscript Printing

Postscript printing allows you to print illustrations created on a program such as Adobe Illustrator and saved in EPS (encapsulated PostScript) format. Some printers have PostScript support built in, while others can be made compatible with the use of software.

Printers and Resolution

The standard for resolution today is 600 × 600dpi (or the equivalent 720 × 720 for some inkjet printers), but you can find both higher and lower resolution. In general, you'll want to avoid lower resolutions unless you get an exceptionally low price and never use anything but 10- or 12-point text. Don't insist on 1,200dpi unless you need high-quality photographic output. Make sure you find out both the vertical and horizontal resolution for any printer you're considering, and bear in mind that many inkjets have different resolutions for colour and monochrome printing.

Resolution isn't the only factor that determines the output quality of your photographic prints. You also need to know whether the printer offers resolution enhancement, and if so, what kind. Edge enhancement typically varies the size or position of dots on edges of lines, text and solid blocks. Because this feature smoothes edges, it can produce an apparent resolution nearly double the dpi rating; however, it won't improve continuous-tone images such as photos. For photos, you can get very different output quality at any given resolution, depending on how the printer creates shades of grey and shades of colours.

The best way to find out how well a printer handles photos is to look at a sample output. If you can't see samples before buying, make sure you can return the printer if you don't like the results.

Photo Printing

If you need to print photos at the highest possible quality, consider an inkjet specifically designed for photos. Such a printer typically offers six ink colours rather than the usual four. The additional two colours improve photo quality in two ways: they increase the range of colours the printers can print, and they decrease the number of individual dots the printers need to create most colours.

Lowering the number of dots is important because it reduces the likelihood of showing noticeable 'dithering' patterns. Because six-colour printers can print any individual dot in more possible colours than four-colour printers, they don't need as many dots to fake other colours. Fewer dots mean smaller, less visible patterns of dots.

Interface

The conventional choice for connecting to a stand-alone system is a parallel port, which is still a good choice, although USB ports are an attractive alternative for quick and easy connections, particularly if you may have to switch the printer between desktop and notebook systems on a regular basis. Of course, before you choose USB, be sure you have a USB port on your computer and that your operating system supports it.

Keep in mind also that as you add more USB devices to a USB chain, the performance of each device can suffer because they all share the same connection. If you're putting the printer on a network, you'll get the best performance with a network connection.

Most printers separate the cost of the network interface from that of the printer because there are so many choices. Just don't forget to add the price of your particular interface into your budget.

Cartridge/Toner Life

Take a look at both the price of an ink or toner cartridge for any given printer and the number of pages it will print. An inexpensive cartridge that prints relatively few pages may actually be much more costly than a more expensive cartridge that prints more pages. Higher-capacity cartridges also mean that you won't have to change them as often, which can be particularly important for a network printer in an office that is used to print a large number of pages.

What warranty is best for me?
Read your warranty carefully. A three-year warranty might appear to be more attractive than a one-year warranty, but the one-year plan might cover parts and labour and the three-year plan might not. Find out who pays for transport on major repairs, and whether you can receive a courtesy model while your scanner or printer is being repaired.

Using the Right Type of Paper

When it comes to printing photographic quality prints, choosing the right paper is very important. The four basic types of paper are:

- *Copier paper:* plain paper or copier paper is the least desirable type of paper for printing photographic images. This paper is OK for printing text, but you'll get a smeared image if you use this paper for printing photos. Because it is less expensive than other papers, it is often a good choice for printing test copies.
- *Inkjet paper:* special inkjet paper is best for printing photographic images. Inkjet paper absorbs ink well and creates a crisp image.
- *Photographic paper:* special photographic paper comes in various sizes and stocks, and it is the best choice for printing photographic images. It absorbs ink very well, but it is also quite expensive. To save money, print a few test images on plain paper before you print a final copy on photographic paper.
- *Other papers:* you can find all types of speciality papers to use for producing stickers, colour transparencies, iron-on transfers, decals, bookmarks and the like. These can be a lot of fun to work with, and can be purchased almost anywhere.

How Long Can I Expect My Prints to Last?

You've decided that a digital camera and inkjet printer might be the best way to get your photographic prints. But how long will the prints last? It is actually light that kills the colour in prints, and ultraviolet light is the worst. The magenta and purple colour dyes in inkjet prints fade the quickest; bright magenta often turns red or brown fairly quickly if it is exposed to sunlight. Modern Epson printers use a dye-based ink system that is predicted to last three to four times longer if the image is printed on Epson paper – in fact, Epson claims that their new inks on their heavyweight matte paper will last for 25 years.

Another way to make your prints last longer is to protect them under UV absorbing glass, which you can find in frame shops. It is estimated that a print that is protected in a low ultraviolet environment could last 30 years or more. And although it's true that the images you print today aren't going to be as colourful ten years from now, the same can be said about traditional photographs.

CHAPTER 19

Improving Your Digital Pictures

Although there is no way to avoid ending up with a few disappointing pictures, there are techniques you can use to minimize the number of bad photos you accumulate. And an exciting aspect of digital photography is that you can use image-editing software to improve, and use, those less-than-perfect images.

Ways to Improve Your Digital Images While Shooting

Today's high-tech digital cameras make it easy for almost anyone to create good photos. With the additional advantage of image-editing software, your satisfaction is practically assured. However, there are some actions you can take while shooting that will improve your images and reduce the need for editing.

Take Time to Compose Your Shot

Just as with traditional analogue photography, good digital photographs rely on certain basic things such as good composition. Many of the techniques of film photography apply to digital photography as well. Strive to get the best possible shot; don't expect to correct all your 'mistakes' later with image-editing software.

Get Close

Most photos miss the mark because the photographer did not get close enough to his or her subject. Your objective should be to fill the frame. This will result in photos that are better composed and provide more visual information to work with when you edit your images with your computer.

Get closer to your subject, or zoom in for tight framing; a closer shot creates a greater sense of intimacy. When shooting vertical images – people, buildings, trees – turn the camera for a vertical orientation, and avoid empty space at the edges of the frame.

Keep It Simple

Avoid clutter in your photos. To do so, change the angle of view or move closer to your subject. Aim for one strong focal point in your composition. Rely more on close-ups and simple compositions, and you will be pleased with the improvements in your photographs.

Experiment with Lighting

Try shooting at different times of day to see the effects on your subjects. Just make sure you never shoot directly into the sun.

Plan Ahead for Action Shots

One drawback to digital cameras is shutter lag. On a film camera, you press the shutter button and the camera snaps the photo almost immediately, usually within a few tenths of a second. On a digital camera, the delay after you press the shutter button (shutter lag) can last as long as a full second. This lag is the result of the time used by the digital camera to focus on the subject, calculate exposure and adjust for proper colour balance.

One way to avoid shutter lag is to prefocus the camera. If you can determine a spot where the action is apt to take place, such as the area around the goal at the end of a football pitch, you can prefocus on that area and wait for the action to occur. On most digital cameras, if you press the shutter button halfway, the camera will begin focusing and adjusting for the proper exposure. Then when you snap the photo, the shutter lag is reduced to only two or three tenths of a second.

If your camera is equipped with a high-speed continuous shooting mode, you can utilize it to quickly snap several shots in a row. But remember that in high-speed mode some cameras capture very low-res images. Check your camera's manual for more information.

Avoid Stiff Portraits

When taking snapshots of a group of people, you'll get better results if they are involved in an activity or are interacting with each other. Allow people to sit or lean against something so they will feel, and look, more relaxed. Make sure you are not catching them squinting into the sun.

Creating Your Digital Darkroom

One of the many advantages of digital photography is the ability for any photographer to create his or her own 'darkroom' with a computer and image-editing software. Although the term 'digital darkroom' is a bit of a misnomer, the benefits of using an image editor are very real – it provides the user with the ability to correct colour, crop, duplicate and retouch images. You can reduce red-eye, adjust contrast, resize objects, make a photo collage, control perspective, distort the photo for a special effect and add text. The darkroom was once the province of the professional photographer, but now almost anyone can use a digital camera, scanner and image-editing software on their home computer to produce high-quality images.

You need a digital camera or a scanner in order to capture digital images. (Scanners are discussed in more detail in Chapter 17.) And you need a computer and an image-editing program in order to manipulate your images.

You can use the image-editing software that came bundled with your camera or scanner to begin your journey into digital editing. Using the software that came with your camera, you should be able to transfer your images to the computer and view thumbnails of them. The scanning software may allow you to carry out some basic manipulating and enhancing actions – you will probably be able to correct the colour, contrast and brightness, among other things.

Often the software that accompanies the digital camera or scanner is not the full version of the commercial product. Once you've become accustomed to using your software, you can decide whether to purchase a program that gives you more options.

Choosing an Image Editor

You can produce some fantastic results when you edit your digital images, but much depends on choosing the right software. There are numerous image-editing software programs on the market, ranging from under £40 to well over £300. How do you sort through all that's available to find the one that's best for you?

When should you purchase image-editing software?
All digital cameras and scanners come packaged with image-editing software. You should start editing your pictures with the software that came with your equipment. Once you have used it for a while and got the hang of the techniques it offers, you'll have a better idea of what to look for when you move up to a more advanced program.

The Right Tools

If you are really serious about wanting to manipulate your digital images, you will need certain editing tools to be able to produce the best results. Listed below are a few tools for maximum control and superior results that you should look for when purchasing your image-editing software.

Precise Selecting Tools

Some programs come with simple rectangular and elliptical lasso tools that are used to select rectangular and elliptical areas of an image for editing. If you are interested in doing more sophisticated image editing, you'll need more sophisticated selecting tools. Look for a custom lasso tool so that you can select any area, regardless of its shape. Colour-based selecting tools are even better.

Layers

When combining images to form photo collages, you will have much more control of the program if each object is assigned to its own layer. Independent objects can be repositioned or deleted without adversely affecting the rest of the image – for example, if you want to utilize a background of brightly coloured autumn trees and place a person in the foreground, layering can allow you to do this. Adjustment layers let you apply colour and make other corrections to an image without changing its original content.

Soft Edge

A soft edge makes the transition between a selection and another area less noticeable. When you paste an element into another image using this tool, the lines of demarcation become less apparent and each one seamlessly blends into another.

Rubber Stamp or Clone Tool

The ability to copy objects is absolutely essential when editing an image. This tool is described in more detail below.

Red-Eye Reduction

Red-eye reduction is a popular tool, since most people at one time or another end up with images that feature eyes of an unnatural colour. The red-eye reduction tool is sometimes difficult to use, so make sure the image editor you buy lets you effortlessly adjust the size and type of colour you're applying to correct red-eye.

Ease of Navigation

In addition to having the tools described above, it is important that your image editor is easy to use. Some inexpensive software programs are loaded with wizards, which take you step by step through the editing process. Although wizards can be useful, they can also impede navigation – for instance, a tool that you might want to use may not be shown in some windows since the wizard has 'simplified' and eliminated the process.

When it comes to file formats, the more your software program can support, the better off you'll be. Some of the most common file formats are JPEG, GIF, TIFF, BMP, EPS and PICT. See Chapter 15 for more information on file formats.

More expensive programs, such as Photoshop, offer less onscreen help but more flexibility, allowing you to choose tools at will so you can make a wide range of manual edits. However, you don't have to invest in Photoshop to get the flexibility you need. Some less expensive programs,

such as PhotoImpact, manage to be easy to navigate while foregoing the use
of limiting wizards.

Web Integration

If you plan to use your digital images on the Internet, you should make sure
that your image-editing software will make it easy for you to do so. Some
programs effectively help you send photos via e-mail, add images to a
webpage, post your images to a website where others can view them, and
transfer your images to online printing services.

It pays to do some research and compare several software programs
before purchasing one. A closer look at some popular image-editing
software programs is taken in Chapter 21.

Overview of Imaging Tools

After you've set up your digital darkroom, you will probably be eager to start
having fun editing your images. But before you jump in, carefully review the
user's guides that came with your hardware and software.

Your software program offers quite a wide array of image manipulation
tools. Take some time to learn about the uses of each tool. Here is an
overview of tools that typically are found in image editors – different
programs have different tools, though there is quite a bit of overlap among
programs. Tools with similar functions often have different names.

- *Airbrush:* sprays colour ('paint') onto the image
- *Blur/sharpen/smudge:* lets you blur or sharpen certain areas
  of an image
- *Burn/dodge/sponge:* lightens or darkens an area of the image
- *Eraser:* eliminates any unwanted area
- *Eyedroppers:* allows you to sample and duplicate a colour from
  an image
- *Gradient:* creates a smooth transition from one colour to another
- *Hand:* moves the image around the screen
- *History brush:* allows you to undo certain areas

- *Lasso:* selects an area of the image
- *Magic wand:* allows you to select pixels based on similar colours
- *Marquee/crop:* allows you to select rectangular and elliptical areas for cropping
- *Measure:* a ruler that measures the image
- *Move:* allows you to move selected areas and layers
- *Paint bucket:* lets you fill specific areas of an image with a particular colour
- *Paintbrush:* allows you to colour your image; has a softer edge than the pencil tool
- *Pencil:* allows you to hand draw or colour; has a harder edge than the paintbrush tool
- *Rubber stamp/cloning tool:* allows you to copy, or clone, parts of an image
- *Type:* lets you add text to the image
- *Zoom:* magnifies the image for easier retouching.

Image-Editing Tips

No matter what image editor you are using, you will get the most from your software with the least amount of frustration if you adhere to the following principles and processes.

Duplicate Your Image

Make at least one copy of your original image, and preserve the original in the same way you would protect a negative from a 35mm camera. Edit the copy. This way, if you end up with results that are unsatisfactory and unsalvageable, you can simply go back and make a new copy of your original and begin again. Because some software programs don't offer multiple undo features, once you have made and saved changes you may not be able to return to your original image.

Always save at least one copy of your original digital image before beginning to work your editing magic on it. Better yet, save two copies. That way if you end up hating what you've done with your image-editing software, you'll always have the option of starting again with a fresh original.

Start with a Quick Fix

Begin by choosing the quick fix or instant fix option. With repeated use, you'll learn whether or not this option tends to make images look better or worse. (The quick fix won't always improve your digital images.) Hopefully, your quick fix option will correct the most obvious problems for you, saving you editing time and effort. Then you can use your editing time to make more precise changes in contrast, colour and the like, as needed.

Remember the Cloning Tool

Users often overlook the cloning tool, yet it can prove to be one of the most powerful tools offered by an image editor. Rid your image of unwanted elements by simply painting over them using the cloning tool. It is also helpful for matching colours.

Try a Soft Touch

The image editor's softening tools can help you blend separate images together. Sharpening images can sometimes result in an artificial look; the softening tools can be very helpful for a more natural image.

Editing Hints for Better Images

Image-editing software is a real boon for the photographer. Now it's a doddle to get creative with your digital photos and produce some astonishing effects. Just remember a few key points:

·   Read the user's guide that came with your image-editing software, then be prepared to do a bit of experimenting in order to fully grasp how the program's tools work.

· Just because you can change something doesn't mean that you should. Don't manipulate your image too much, or it can end up being too much of a good thing. For best results, change only a few key elements. A light touch is best.

· Remember that a low-resolution image cannot be enlarged without some loss of quality.

· Read up on digital imagery and its manipulation to find out how particular effects are accomplished. Visit your local library or bookshop for books and magazines, or search the Internet for how-to articles on digital photography.

The Power of Editing Tools

Just as photographers have long used the darkroom to control the final processing of film, your image editor allows you to manipulate your digital image, controlling the final output. A software program saves you the hours you would have spent in a traditional darkroom, and offers many other advantages as well. You can correct your image by adjusting and improving the colour, composition and brightness. You can resize your photo, apply special effects and even turn it into a painting. Professional-level software programs offer literally thousands of different options for the digital photographer seeking to creatively manipulate an image. Other simpler programs focus on ease of use, allowing you to jump right into a project without having to develop the knowledge and technique of a graphics professional.

Chapter 21 examines in detail specific image-editing software programs of various levels and price points. For now, let's explore some of the tools that image editors commonly provide and the resulting techniques you can utilize to improve images.

Correcting Your Digital Images

You can make an endless number of improvements to your digital photos using an image editor. Here are just a few common problems and the techniques you can use to solve them.

Changing Format

Some subjects lend themselves to vertical orientation; others look better when taken in the horizontal format. In general, people and buildings tend to look better when taken in the vertical format, while landscapes and groups of people work well with the horizontal format.

Because landscapes are often shot in horizontal format, such orientation is usually referred to as 'landscape format'. And because portraits are often shot in a vertical format, such orientation is generally referred to as 'portrait format'.

If you find you've taken a photo of a building in the horizontal format and you'd like to change it to vertical, you can select the area you want to work with and then crop away the rest. Using this approach, it becomes easy to salvage an image by changing its format.

Correcting Colour

Your digital camera likely has a colour balance setting that makes adjustments for colours that are too warm or too cool. In the same way, image-editing software also utilizes colour balance for better pictures.

Another way you can adjust colour in your image is by changing the saturation. Doing so allows you to boost colours or make them more subdued.

Correcting Converging Verticals

The problem of converging verticals frequently happens when the photographer uses a wide-angle lens and looks up to shoot a building. In the resulting photo, it looks as if the building is tipping backwards. With a film camera, there is no easy solution to this problem, but digital image editors can do the job quickly.

To fix the problem of converging verticals, the top of the original image is stretched until all vertical lines appear upright, then the image is cropped to fit inside a rectangle. There are other minor adjustments that might need to be made, but they can be accomplished quite quickly. By correcting converging verticals, you'll be left with a more realistic image of a building – one that is firmly planted on the ground.

Combining Images

Have you ever wished you could take the best parts of two (or more) pictures and merge them? Now you can. Simply use your editing program to copy the element you want to use as a substitute and save it at the same resolution as the base image you're using. Shape it to fit, place it into position then blend it so that it appears as if it had always been there.

Combining images works particularly well with pictures of people. For instance, let's say you want to capture a picture of your friend Maria talking to her son, Joseph. You've got one shot where Maria looks great, but Joseph has his eyes closed. In the second photo Joseph has a sunny smile, but Maria is looking away from the camera. Simply take the smiling Joseph and add it to the shot where Maria is facing the camera, and you've got a winning photo.

Improving Sharpness

Because of the technology used to capture them, digital images have a tendency to appear fuzzy. Usually the problem is easily corrected by using the automatic sharpening mode. However, sometimes a picture may need extra help.

To add crispness, begin by applying the unsharp masking technique to enhance contrast, then use the sharpening tool to bring the image into focus. Just be careful not to get carried away with sharpening, or your image could end up looking unnatural. As with other image-editing tools, a light hand usually provides the best results.

Getting Rid of Red-Eye

Red-eye typically occurs in low-light situations – the pupils of the subject dilate to let in light, and when the flash fires, it reflects off the blood vessels at the back of the eye. The result: the subject's eyes appear bright red. Some software programs feature an easy-to-use red-eye reduction mode. If your program doesn't offer an automatic red-eye reduction option, you can enlarge the image and paint over the red with the desired eye colour.

Refining the Background

As discussed in Chapters 11 and 12, our eyes automatically screen out a lot of the clutter that surrounds us in our everyday lives. That's why when we're busy taking pictures in the field we don't always realize what the background will look like in the finished photo. By using software to change the background of a picture, we can transform it from tiresome to spectacular.

This is another process that requires scrupulous attention to detail as you cut out your image, clean it up, save it and add it to the background of your choice. You may want to start collecting interesting backgrounds for use as the need arises. Some software programs provide a variety of backgrounds to help you get your image bank started.

Another way to approach changing a background is to isolate the main element in your picture, keeping it sharp while you blur the background. You can even move your subject's position in the frame, perhaps putting more emphasis on the foreground.

Shooting Images with a Specific Purpose in Mind

As you become more adept with your image editor, you may want to experiment with different techniques. One good habit to get into is to keep an eye out for interesting backgrounds that can be used later to enhance shots where the subject is interesting but the background is cluttered or bland – images with interesting views of the sky, a row of trees or skylines are all possible backgrounds. If you enjoy creating collages, always keep an eye open for subjects that could be utilized as elements for compositions. One of the interesting aspects of digital photography is the ability to combine photos. By compiling an image bank, you'll be assured of always having plenty of material to draw on.

CHAPTER 20

Getting Creative With Digital Images

This chapter takes a look at the effects you can create using image editors, plus other imaginative ways to have fun with your digital images. It examines darkroom techniques you can do on your computer, such as embossing, burning, cropping, duotones, flipping and many others, and then looks into how to get camera-like results from your software. The range of artistic and special effects available grows every day, and there seems to be no end to the possibilities that await you in your digital darkroom.

Replacing the Traditional Darkroom

In the digital world, certain tasks previously undertaken in the darkroom using chemicals are now executed with a computer and software. Here are some of the most common tasks you can perform with your image editor.

- *Adjusting brightness*: allows you to lighten or darken your image without affecting the colour balance or overall contrast.
- *Burning/dodging/sponging*: burning darkens an image, dodging lightens it, and sponging increases or decreases the saturation of colours. All of these techniques took the traditional film photographer hours of work in the darkroom. With an image editor, you can lighten or darken your photo far more quickly and easily.
- *Colour correction*: using an image editor, you can make fine adjustments to the hue, saturation, colour balance and brightness of your image. You can even substitute one colour for another wherever the colour to be changed appears.
- *Adjusting contrast range*: you can choose to include more or less detail in your image by adjusting the difference between the lightest and darkest parts of an image (contrast range). By manipulating the contrast range and brightness, you can often salvage an overexposed or underexposed image.
- *Cropping*: even simple image editors allow you to change the shape or printing size of your image.
- *Creating duotones*: these are created in a traditional darkroom by tinting a black-and-white photograph. The grey area in the photo turns a particular tint, such as sepia, while black stays black and white remains white.
- *Hand colouring*: before the introduction of colour film, hand colouring was a popular way to add colour to a black-and-white print. Today, modern image-editing software allows you to 'hand colour' your photo using painting tools.
- *Inverting*: the invert command lets you instantly turn a positive image into a negative image, and vice versa.

- *Creating lithographic effects*: lithographic film produces extremely high-contrast photographs, reducing monochromatic images to pure black and white. Now, instead of creating these results in the darkroom, you can use an image editor to easily produce dramatic images of high contrast.
- *Masking*: the masking tool preserves areas of an image, in the same way that a dust sheet protects your furniture while you paint a room. Masking permits you to apply an effect to one specific part of an image or to vary the strength of an effect within an image.
- *Posterization*: in a traditional darkroom, a posterized image was created by replacing shading and gradations of tone with marked changes in colour. It was accomplished through an elaborate process using multiple negatives printed at varied exposures and contrasts. Image-editing software enables you to achieve this effect without the time and element of risk.
- *Reticulation*: when 35mm film is processed incorrectly, an effect called reticulation can occur, resulting in a photo that appears very grainy. Using an image editor, you can deliberately achieve a similar effect with your digital images.
- *Retouching*: with an image editor, you can retouch any digital image using a variety of tools and techniques. Retouching allows you to remove dust, scratches and blemishes, and is a common feature of image-editing software programs.
- *Solarization*: in the traditional darkroom, solarization is the term used to describe the reversed tones of a photographic image that result from prolonged exposure to an extremely bright light. What once took hours of experimentation in the darkroom can now be created using the curves feature in an image-editing software program.

Solarization, also known as the Sabbatier effect, is the term used to describe the reversed tones of a photographic image. In the 19th century Sabbatier discovered that exposing photosensitive materials to a bright light for prolonged periods caused some of the tones to reverse.

Camera-like Results

Image-editing software is not a replacement for a good photographer. However, it can provide some effects that in the past were attained only when a photographer employed certain techniques while shooting.

Blur/Focus

A photographer manipulates the shutter speed and aperture while shooting in order to create a desired effect in a photograph. Sometimes he or she will deliberately produce a blurry image to suggest a particular mood; at other times, he or she will choose to have a photo sharply focused. You can get similar results using an image editor – for instance, you can decide to blur the whole image or just a specific area of it.

Software programs offer different types of blur, including random, which creates a general fuzziness, and motion, which is similar to the effect achieved when panning a camera. You can also specify the degree to which you want the image blurred.

Filters

In film photography, a filter is attached over the camera's lens in order to alter the light before it reaches the film. In digital photography, the term 'filter' refers to an effect achieved by an image editor on a digital image. Digital filters change the effects on your images, frequently in a different manner from traditional photographic filters. Filters may come with your software program or as plug-ins.

There are two general types of filters: those that improve the quality of images, and those that allow you to be creative and add special effects. The following sections explore some of the creative effects you can apply using image-editing software.

Artistic Effects

There are many artistic effects that you can achieve using an image editor. Image-editing software programs commonly allow the user to choose 'painting' tools, such as a pointed or flat brush tip, an airbrush or spray paint; you may also be given your choice of medium, from pencil and ink to crayons, chalk and pastels. But some of the most interesting effects are achieved through the use of special filters – you can try your hand with different filters and achieve masterly results without having to take expensive and time-consuming art classes. Below are five special filters and the results they provide.

· *Contouring filter:* contour drawing refers to drawing just the outline (contour) of a subject. When you apply contouring to your digital images, the results will vary widely, depending on the photos you're using.

· *Mosaic/tile filter:* the mosaic filter enlarges the size of the pixels in your digital image so that they resemble tiles in a mosaic, creating an image that is somewhat abstract but still discernible. The user can adjust the size of the pixels to vary the effect.

· *Oil painting/palette knife filter:* the palette knife filter gives your photo the look of an oil painting. You can significantly change the effect by selecting a different 'brushstroke' size.

· *Pointillist filter:* if you have always admired the work of the famous French artist Georges Seurat, who rendered pictures by painting a series of small dots of paint, you may enjoy using a filter that will cause your digital image to mimic an impressionistic pointillist painting. More sophisticated programs allow you to decide the size and colour of the dots and how they are dispersed. This filter requires a bit of experimentation in order to achieve the best results.

· *Watercolour filter:* if you'd prefer an image that mimics a watercolour painting, choose the watercolour filter. It works especially well with subjects from nature, but use it sparingly for an aethereal feeling.

Collage/Montage/Composite

Using photographic software, it's fun to mix images to create unique effects. Whether you call it a collage, montage or composite, a collection of different photos grouped together to form one image can be a visually appealing way to tell a story. As part of your collage you can include artwork and text, as well as images.

A collage is not an easy project to execute; it requires far more than simply assembling miscellaneous images. To create a collage that works, you need a good eye for composition, some practice using your software program and, most importantly, an engaging concept. The images in a collage should have a thread or theme that connects them so that they work together to convey one particular idea or impression.

Top-level programs enable you to assign weights to the various images in your collage so that certain objects appear more prominent while others seem to recede. You can also choose the transparency of various objects and the extent to which the edges of photos blend together.

Don't overlook the value of using stock photography in combination with your digital images. Let's say you want to create a collage, and in your mind you picture a beautiful sunflower in front of a red barn. With stock photography, you can search for just the image you need.

Special Effects

Besides the effects achievable with image-editing software that have been discussed so far, there are many other possibilities. Read on to learn more about the amazing results you can achieve with a little imagination and your own digital images.

Distortion/Warping

Some image-editing software programs allow you to distort and stretch an image for unusual effects. A program may offer you the ability to choose the shape and axes of the distortion, the rate of distortion and the precise area of the image that will be distorted. There are several types of distortion, each with its own effects:

- *Linear:* using linear distortion, your image is stretched on the horizontal axis or the vertical axis, or on a diagonal.
- *Pinch:* also known as thinning or imploding, this technique 'pinches' the image in.
- *Spherical:* also referred to as fat effects or exploding, spherical distortion 'puffs' out the photo at whatever point the user specifies, following a circular pattern. This effect is similar to that provided by a fish-eye lens on a film camera.
- *Stretch or goo:* some programs allow you to simply click on an area of your image and drag the mouse to give the appearance of stretching the image. It is almost as if you are working with an image made of Potty Putty or rubber.

Adding Text

The ability to add text to an image may seem to be a feature that would appeal only to those using image editors for professional uses, such as composing advertisements or catalogues. But you may find that a word or two can make a nice addition to your digital picture. The text tool makes it simple to add type – consider using it to designate the place shown in a travel photo, to reveal the name of the subject captured in your portrait, or as an added element in a collage.

From Colour to Monochrome

With film cameras, you must decide before shooting whether you want your pictures to be black and white or colour; one of the great advantages of digital photography is the freedom it offers in this area. After capturing your digital image in colour, you can decide to change it to a monochromatic one by copying it and saving it as a monochrome image. The same effect can be achieved on a photographic print that has been scanned and downloaded to your computer.

Infrared Effects

Film photographers obtain unexpected results with infrared film. Infrared film is sensitive to both the light that humans can see and some of the longer-length infrared radiation that cannot be seen with the naked eye. It takes time, experimentation and considerable effort to use infrared film effectively. FIGURE 20-1 shows an infrared photograph taken with a film camera.

FIGURE 20-1:
This is an example of an infrared photograph taken with a film camera.

Photo by Philip Thornberry

A similar result can be obtained with digital photos and an image editor. If you choose your subject carefully, you can manipulate the hue and saturation to achieve results similar to infrared photos.

Patterns

Chapter 11 talked about capturing patterns while shooting. Another way to have fun with patterns is to create them using your computer – find an element of your image that is appealing to you, then experiment with creative ways of duplicating and using it. For best results, you need to pay particular attention to detail when combining the repeated elements so that they blend perfectly together.

Reflections/Mirror Images

One way to use patterns imaginatively is to create images that contain mirror images, or reflections. Start with an image that is strong enough to stand alone and still be effective, then experiment with duplicating it by copying it onto its own layer and flipping it – combining the two images results in a mirror image. You can also be creative with this technique by mixing several images at once to form repeating patterns or multiple reflections.

The glowing edges filter is used to transform your image into a tracery of neon-like lines by defining the edges in your photo and reversing their tones and colours.

Ripple Filter

Imagine tossing a stone into a still body of water and watching ripples appear on the water's surface. In the same way that ripples become visible in water, distorting the reflections on the water's surface, the ripple filter produces a distorting effect on an image. There are a number of controls you can use to cause a range of effects, from slight rippling to maximum distortion. When using the ripple filter, you will need to choose your subject wisely in order to obtain satisfactory results.

Twirl Filter

When you're looking for a different way to distort an image and create a unique effect, apply the twirl filter, which twists an image around its centre either clockwise or anticlockwise, depending on which you specify; you also control the degree to which your image is twirled. The final result is an interesting spiral distortion of the original image.

Silhouetting/Vignetting

It used to be the case that negatives were painted to create a white silhouette, or border, around the edges of the picture. Many software programs allow you to apply this masking function to your digital images, imparting a vintage look. The technique works best on simple images, especially portraits. Consider scanning an old photo then adding sepia tones and a vignette effect to recreate the charm of a bygone era.

Having Fun With Your Photos

Photography has always been a creative medium, but digital technology provides even more opportunities for you to unleash the power of your imagination. Consider these possibilities, then see what enjoyable things you can do with your digital images.

It's easy to execute photo projects using ClickArt 300,000 Premier Image Pak from Broderbund – you can create posters, stationery, invitations, greeting cards, banners, pamphlets, letterheads, newsletters, brochures, school projects, webpages and lots of other items using the program's step-by-step instructions. The package includes 160,000 high-quality images and graphics, 50,000 photos and 20,000 illustrations, 60,000 Internet graphics, 7,000 sounds and 2,500 fonts, so you're sure to have all the tools you need. ClickArt 300,000 is available for about £70.

Getting Children into the Act

Children will love playing around with digital images just as much as you do. In fact, because they tend to be less inhibited than adults, especially when working with computers, they may have more fun with photographic software than you do.

There are special photography software programs designed specifically for children. If you have an easy-to-use general consumer image editor, your older children will probably be able to use it to produce some exciting results once they've had a little practice.

Schoolchildren can incorporate digital images into their reports, research work, special projects and other school work. If you don't have an image editor or layout program at home, a word processor should be enough to produce what's needed. Photos and text can be combined in the program, and by varying the font and point size of the text, the student can produce some eye-catching results.

If you have children from the age of six up, Looney Tunes PhotoFun software can keep them busy for hours with projects ranging from making cards and badges to using their own images in ready-made scenes. They'll also be amused by the Looney Tunes characters that walk them through each activity. The program, which is manufactured by MGI Software, costs about £25, but it's worth shopping around for this, as well as some of the other programs here.

Adding a Border or Frame

Today's children bring home some fantastic school pictures, but now you don't have to rely on a professional photographer to get outstanding pictures of the children in your life. With your digital camera and the right software, you can create your own jazzy pictures. One trick to take advantage of is the inclusion of a border or frame directly in the image. You can pick a frame that looks like real wood, one that seems like it's been drawn with a crayon or a stained-glass design, or choose from a wide variety of other patterns and colours to complement or contrast with your photo. When framing children's photos, why not let them have a say in choosing the frame? And don't forget to print out extras, because grandparents and other relatives are going to want copies.

Turning Digital Images Into Gifts

Your digital images don't have to remain photos: there are software programs on the market that make it easy to create novelty items and gifts that incorporate your images – photos are no longer simply for use in holiday cards. With the increased popularity of digital photography, images can now be incorporated into any number of items, including:

- Calendars and buttons
- T-shirts
- Wrapping paper
- Picture cubes
- Stationery, cards and stickers

If you do decide to try your hand at turning your photos into wrapping paper and you're using an inkjet printer, you might want to pick up some fixative at an art supply store. This will keep your design from smearing or rubbing off.

Digital Photographs: Other Good Uses

Putting Digital Images to Work

If you're a small business owner or are self-employed, a digital camera can be a wise investment and is probably tax-deductible. Digital images can be put to good use at work: for instance, you can add interest to your newsletter, whether your target audience is your own staff, prospective clients or current customers. Using a digital camera, you can take pictures of office parties, the annual company picnic or new employees, then incorporate your snapshots in the next employee newsletter. If you have an in-house design or creative department, staff there can manipulate the images for a wide variety of uses. Product shots can be incorporated into newsletters, product sell sheets, slide show presentations and more.

Some businesses, in particular, really benefit from going digital – for example, estate agents can employ pictures of homes to motivate potential buyers, as a photo of a home is the perfect addition to a sell sheet distributed or displayed.

An insurance agent can use a digital camera to snap a picture of a damaged vehicle or building, then e-mail the image to others for a quick way to share information that applies to a claim.

Anyone working in communications, whether a public relations specialist, freelance writer or news reporter, can benefit from having a digital camera handy to capture an important moment in time.

Digital images can be a powerful way to tell a story about a company, product, person or event. People love pictures, and digital images can really spice up your business communications.

PhotoParade Maker 5.0 makes it easy to enjoy your digital images every day. This software package allows you to turn your favourite images into a screen saver or wallpaper for your computer, or create a photo slide show that you can e-mail to family and friends. PhotoParade Maker comes bundled with an assortment of themes to complement your photos, and a free downloadable PhotoParade Player means anyone can view your PhotoParade. See *www.photoparade.com* for more details.

If you're a Palm Pilot user, take advantage of some of the free programs that turn your Palm into a photo album. PhotoAlbum 3, manufactured by Corel, is available for downloading at *www.photoalb.com*. Using PhotoAlbum 3, you can turn your Palm Pilot into a photo album, displaying black-and-white images as either high contrast (black-and-white) or greyscale. For users of Microsoft Windows 3.x, 95, 98 and XP, PhotoAlbum Studio version 3.23 is available at *www.microsoft.com*. This freeware utility lets you create your own Palm Pilot photo albums from your BMP files.

Using Digital Images at School, Organizations and More

Teachers and others who work in schools will find endless opportunities to use digital snapshots. One mother of four related to me that her child's teacher used digital pictures to create a newsletter that was sent home with the children on the second day of the new school year. The newsletter featured the headline 'They're Back!' and showed a picture of the class taken on the first day of the new term.

She also reported that the weekly and monthly newsletters that her children bring home from school have become a lot more interesting since the teachers began adding pictures to them. For example, when a special guest comes to the classroom, the newsletter describes the event and shows a photo of the guest talking to the children, which gives parents a bird's-eye view into their children's classrooms.

Students working on school projects and newspapers are embracing digital photography as a means of catching the action wherever and whenever it happens – at sporting events, in the classroom, on field trips and at social events. They can use graphic design software programs to manipulate their images and combine them with text for top-notch results.

Scout and Guide leaders and others who work with children in volunteer capacities can achieve similar results with a computer and a digital camera or scanner. Bulletins, flyers and invitations can display photos of the children in action and show off some of the projects they're working on. Even announcements of upcoming fund-raising events, such as car boot sales, can entice participation by displaying pictures of the goods that will be on offer.

CHAPTER 21

Image-Editing Software

As the popularity of digital photography skyrockets, the number of available software programs is also growing at a fast rate. Because image editors allow consumers to turn their computers into digital darkrooms, even amateur photographers can experience the pleasure that comes from working with digital images. You can use image-editing software to touch up pictures, but you can go far beyond simply eliminating red-eye and cropping photos.

Overview of Image-Editing Programs

The most powerful program on the market is Adobe's Photoshop – Adobe calls Photoshop the world standard image editor, and everyone else seems to agree. Graphics professionals know the power of Photoshop because they use it on a daily basis, but if you're an amateur photographer, jumping into Photoshop as your first image editor is like jumping into a Ferrari when all you really need is a good economy car to take you around town.

Remember that as you spend more money, you will get a more sophisticated program with additional bells and whistles. To utilize a professional program such as Photoshop will require additional time spent learning how it operates – you may even have to invest money in joining a class or workshop to get the hang of using it.

Magic Series's MagicJpgHtmlPager enables you to create an online photo album, and because it's shareware you can try it without paying a penny. It's easy to make digital photo albums for the Internet or CD-Rs, as the program takes you step by step through the creation process. To download the shareware, go to *www.downseek.com*.

On the other hand, an inexpensive image editor costing less than £80 can often deliver enough options to satisfy the beginning digital photographer. Later in this chapter we'll explore some of the popular software programs out there, ranging from the top-of-the-line, but pricey, Photoshop to effective programs with much lower prices.

Questions to Ask When Choosing Consumer-Level Software

Before you go shopping for software, take some time to consider your needs. When choosing image-editing software, ask yourself the following questions to help you decide which one is right for you:

·   How will you use the software program? Because technology changes so fast and software programs are constantly being upgraded, think in terms of your short-term needs. Do you want to create pictures for use on a website? E-mail photos to friends? Print images that are good enough to be considered fine art?

· How easy is it to use? The program should be intuitive and easy to operate. If not, you will spend more time learning how to use it.

· What are the program's capabilities? Can it do what you need it to do?

· How much does the program cost? To save money, consider buying through a mail-order or Internet retailer who can offer reduced prices, because once you've purchased the product you'll be turning to the manufacturer for support services. If your local computer retailer offers used equipment, you may find a bargain on the software program you're seeking. Finally, remember that freeware and shareware image-editing programs can be excellent, so don't overlook them.

· What platform is it compatible with? Some software programs are only available for a specific platform (Mac or PC). Pay attention to the system requirements, as some packages list both minimum and recommended system requirements. Remember that if your system has only the minimum requirements, you may run into difficulties when manipulating large image files, and you may need to upgrade your computer's memory or even move up to a more powerful system.

· What file formats does the program support? Most image editors handle the popular image file formats, such as TIFF, JPEG and BMP, but not all programs work with Kodak's Photo CD. To be certain that the program you're considering can support the file formats of your choice, read the package specifications carefully or check the manufacturer's website for complete details.

· Does the program include templates to help you get up to a decent operating speed quickly?

· Does the software program accept Photoshop-compatible plug-ins, which allow you to customize an image editor? If your program supports plug-ins, you'll benefit from more options.

If at all possible, you should try the program before you buy it; this has become more easy to do as more and more manufacturers are offering trial or demo versions of software. Many demo programs are accompanied by magazines and books. Contact the software's manufacturer or visit their website to learn more about demos and trial versions. (See Appendix B for a list of manufacturer websites.)

Can I try out software programs before I buy?
Many software manufacturers provide free trial versions. You can often download the program from their site and try it out at home before you buy. Keep in mind that the demo versions of some of the more sophisticated programs can take up a lot of memory, so you might want to go with a shareware program.

Advanced Image-Editing Software Programs

Let's look at some high-end image editors, beginning with the top of the line, Photoshop.

Adobe Photoshop 7.0 CS

- The king of image-editing programs
- Available for Windows or Macintosh

Adobe Photoshop 7.0 CS represents a major upgrade to the reigning king of image-editing programs. It is the most expensive image-manipulation software program available and can be obtained for about £500, but an upgrade from an earlier version of Photoshop should cost little more than £100 if you look around.

If you're using Photoshop, you get very little handholding, because this is a program designed for professionals. If you are a serious photographer, you may want to consider investing the time, money and effort it will take to learn how to master Photoshop. (It's good to note, however, that the 7.0 edition of Photoshop has been enhanced to make it somewhat easier for novices to comprehend.)

The latest version of Photoshop has dozens of new features, many of which are particularly beneficial to the digital photographer. For instance, when you're cropping an image, you'll appreciate being able to dim the areas of the image that you're about to crop off so that you can have a better idea of how your final image will appear. Other updates include enhanced layer controls, great typographic control, additional tools for publishing to the Internet and a more user-friendly interface.

If you're an amateur digital photographer who looks to do only occasional retouching of images, you may not need – or want – all the power that Photoshop delivers. Check some of the less complicated programs discussed later in this chapter.

No matter how long you work with Photoshop, it seems there are always new ways to use this multidimensional program. The Photo FX section is of particular interest to digital photographers, as it provides tips and tricks for achieving special effects with digital images with a click of your mouse, you can learn how to give your photo a vintage look, create a vignette and more. Novice Photoshop users can find help in the beginner's section, while the Interfaces section provides instructions on achieving the look of wires, screws and more unusual elements.

For more details on Photoshop, visit the manufacturer's website at *www.adobe.co.uk.*

Users of Adobe Photoshop, Corel Photo paint and other software products can benefit from a trip to *www.unleash.com.* This site is loaded with tips and tutorials to help you find your way around many software programs.

Corel Photo Paint 9

- A powerful image-editing and painting program costing much less than Photoshop
- Available only for Windows

If you approach digital photography in the same way that a painter approaches a blank canvas, you should consider Corel Photo Paint 9. This powerful software program provides precise editing capabilities plus the creative tools you need to produce masterpieces. Because Photo Paint 9 is loaded with features and tools, you can quickly produce excellent results. Photo Paint 9 includes a media asset-management tool, a font-management tool, 1,500 photos, 1,200 clip-art images, 1,500 floating objects and 800 fonts.

Photo Paint makes it simple to add special effects to your photos. With more than 100 effects filters, including artistic brushes and texture-based effects, plus multiple onscreen colour palettes, it's easy to turn your digital images into works of art. The program's touch-up tools allow you to effortlessly manipulate your images – choose from sharpen, blend, dodge/burn, tint, sponge, contrast, brightness, hue, smear, smudge and more. Photo Paint also offers users 28 paint modes for superior touching-up applications.

Photo Paint can be found for under £280. More details about the program can be found on the manufacturer's website, *www.corel.com*. Corel also offers the Photo Paint 9 Digital Camera Edition – see the section 'Beginner Programs' later in this chapter for more details.

Intermediate Programs

If you're not a professional photographer or graphic artist, your needs will probably be met by a less sophisticated image-editing program than Adobe Photoshop or Corel Photo Paint. In fact, having to learn how to operate all the bells and whistles of a top-of-the-line image editor can be frustrating for someone who really doesn't need that much power. Many experts recommend starting with a simpler program, and then moving up as your needs change and your skills grow.

Below are descriptions of several intermediate-level software programs that are popular with digital photographers.

Ulead PhotoImpact XL

- An image-editing program with superior features at a reasonable price
- Available only for Windows

Ulead PhotoImpact XL is an advanced image editor with a host of features found in top-of-the-line Adobe Photoshop – at about a fifth of the cost. Digital photographers will find that PhotoImpact XL is an elaborate, powerful software program that offers an array of imaging and painting tools.

PhotoImpact offers the user plenty of control while manipulating images. Besides many standard image-editing tools, PhotoImpact includes exceptional capabilities and tools, such as spin buttons, a colourizing pen, a colour replacement pen, object erasers, a Bezier selection tool, the ability to record macros and multiple undo. The paint eraser tool makes it simple to remove pixels using brushstrokes; to remove pixels of a similar colour, choose the magic eraser.

For those new to the world of digital photography and editing, mastering the wealth of features offered by PhotoImpact XL can be a bit of a challenge. But it you're looking for a program whose value will continue to grow with time, PhotoImpact is a good choice. PhotoImpact's suggested price is £75, and you can download a free, 30-day trial version of PhotoImpact from Ulead's website (*www.ulead.co.uk*).

Adobe Photoshop Elements 2.0

- Digital photographers, this Adobe's for you – the power of Photoshop for less than £100
- Available for Windows or Macintosh

Designed with digital photographers in mind, Photoshop Elements brings you the power of Photoshop at a fraction of the price. And it won't take you weeks of experimenting and training to learn how to operate this midlevel package. With the assistance of Photoshop Elements, you can capture, edit, e-mail and print images – even post them on a website.

You can't work in CMYK mode in Photoshop Elements; however, you do have the option of opening such files and converting them to RGB. Photoshop Elements does allow you to work with EPS files.

Photoshop Elements can be obtained for about £80. Go to *www.adobe.co.uk* for more information about this product.

Jasc Software's Paint Shop Pro 8

· A powerful, affordable image editor
· Available only for Windows

With some 20 million users, you know Paint Shop Pro must be doing something right. This image-editing software is an affordable means of enhancing your digital images. You can easily retouch images using its automatic photo-enhancement features – whether you're creating a print or Internet graphic project, Paint Shop Pro has something to offer. Choose from the program's 75 special effects, and as part of the package, you also get Animation Shop 3, so you can create your own animations.

Paint Shop Pro 8 supports almost 50 file formats. The customizable autosave helps to protect important projects. Paint Shop Pro 8 has a suggested retail price of about £100. Find out more at *www.jasc.com*.

Beginner Programs

There are many beginning photo-editing programs that work well with digital images. You don't need a big budget to start having fun with your images, as the programs listed here show. Even many of the less expensive image editors now pack quite a punch, and you'll be able to take advantage of lots of editing tools and filters.

Microsoft Picture It! Photo Premium Edition 2001

· An easy-to-use editing program with plenty of digital photo tools and filters, plus an extensive image library
· Available only for Windows

This popular photo-editing program has been enhanced with an accessible interface that captures the feel of a website. You operate the Picture It! program using both website-like rollover buttons and hyperlinks and standard dialog boxes and menus. Step-by-step instructions and pop-up tutorials guide the user through Picture It!, making it simple for novices to operate.

For amateur digital photographers who are looking for the best way to store their digital images, the Picture It! program offers a Gallery feature that provides helpful cataloguing functions. You can organize files by customizing categories and applying keywords.

Picture It! works well with web-based projects and tasks, including sending photos via e-mail, ordering reprints from online processing sites and adding photos to websites. The suggested retail price for Picture It! is £60. Learn more at the Microsoft website *(www.microsoft.com)*.

Corel Photo Paint 9 Digital Camera Edition

· A scaled-down version of Photo Paint designed especially for the digital camera user
· Available only for Windows

The award-winning Photo Paint 9 technology is available in Corel's Photo Paint 9 Digital Camera Edition, a version meant specifically for digital photographers. Just like its big brother, the digital camera version includes an 'ixla digital camera interface' that works with more than 120 different models of digital camera. No digital camera? Corel's Photo Paint 9 Digital Camera Edition can be utilized with images from scanners, CDs or the Internet.

The program's suggested retail price is £50. For more information, visit the Corel website *(www.corel.com)*.

MGI PhotoSuite 4 Platinum Edition

- Simple yet powerful photo software that makes it easy to edit, enhance, organize and share digital images
- Available only for Windows

The PhotoSuite line of products from MGI Software has been recognized with more than 75 awards. The standard version, PhotoSuite 4, permits the digital photographer to transfer images from many popular models of digital cameras, a hard drive, CD-ROM, floppy disk or the Internet. You can also use a standard TWAIN connection.

Even though PhotoSuite is a program that is loaded with features, it's easy for beginners to navigate, thanks to the easy-to-follow, step-by-step guides that show you just how to go about completing projects.

With a suggested price of £25, PhotoSuite 4 Platinum Edition's many features make it a real bargain.

ArcSoft's PhotoStudio 5.5

- A powerful photo-editing application with an extensive collection of editing and retouching tools
- Available for Windows only

PhotoStudio offers Windows users a robust editing program at a very reasonable price. Take advantage of its large collection of features and special effects to retouch and enhance your digital images. In addition to offering limitless levels of modification, PhotoStudio includes many features found in top-level programs, such as batch processing, image management, multiple undo and macros. Transfer images to PhotoStudio from your digital camera or scanner, a disk drive or your desktop.

PhotoStudio 5.5 can be found for about £50. A 30-day free trial download is available at the manufacturer's website *(www.arcsoft.com)* and at *www.photoisland.com.*

CHAPTER 22

Using the Web

The beauty of digital images is that they can be transported and shared easily via the Internet. Now, within minutes of shooting your photos, you can get them online and share them with dozens, or even hundreds, of people. You can attach digital photos or digital video clips to e-mail and share your images with anyone who has Internet access. When e-mailing digital photos, it's a good idea to size them at 100 x 150mm (4 x 6in) and 75dpi.

Taking Your Images Online

A friend recently told me the story of how digital photography played a part in announcing her nephew's birth. Within an hour or so after he arrived, the proud father had snapped a picture of the new baby and e-mailed it to faraway relatives and friends. Not only could they get a firsthand look at the newest member of the family and feel part of the happy occasion, but they also could turn around and show off little Alexander by forwarding his digital picture to others.

This is just one example of how digital photography can offer benefits that film photography cannot match. In the past, the only immediate gratification one could hope for came from using Polaroid cameras and film. Using the same example of a baby's arrival, you could snap a Polaroid at the hospital and pass it around, but how could you share it with loved ones in other parts of the world? The chances are that you would have had to rely on the post, which would mean a delay of at least a few days. In the 21st century, photo sharing is a whole new game, thanks to the ever-increasing popularity of digital photography, coupled with the technology of the Internet. Now people all over the globe can communicate and share pictures in moments.

E-mailing Photos

If you enjoy sharing photos, you may want to take advantage of the Internet to create your own personal website where others can view your photo collection.

There are two ways to e-mail digital images: as attachments to your e-mail, or included in the body of the e-mail. Following is a look at both options.

With many e-mail programs, such as those that utilize Outlook Express, e-mailing a digital image can be done in just four simple steps.

When sending your digital photo as an attachment, follow these steps:

1. Open your e-mail program
2. Choose New Mail (or similar)

3. Choose Insert>File
4. Select the image file you wish to send.

When sending your digital photo in the body of an e-mail message, follow these steps:

1. Open your e-mail program
2. Choose New Mail (or similar)
3. Choose Insert>Picture
4. Select the image file you wish to send.

Using the software that came with your digital camera to e-mail your photos can be the simplest method of all.

1. Select an image
2. Choose Send To>Mail Recipient
3. Your e-mail application launches automatically and attaches the digital image file
4. Enter your message, then send it.

Taking Your Photos Online

To take your photo album online, follow these steps:

1. Use your camera to snap pictures, or scan prints, then upload the images to your computer
2. Using your image-editing program, reduce their size and resolution so they will load more quickly
3. Using photo album software, organize the images in one folder
4. Add captions to each picture
5. Upload your photo album to the Internet, following the instructions that came with your album software
6. To make sure the upload was successful, double-check all links and images.

Developing a Family or Genealogy Website

Individuals who are interested in genealogy are finding that a digital camera comes in handy for preserving photos of ancestors, information on headstones and other items of interest, including family heirlooms such as documents, marriage certificates and Bible records. When travelling for work, pleasure or on holiday, an amateur genealogist can use a digital camera to record photos of ancestral homes and other places of interest. The photos captured during genealogical searches can be shared via e-mail or posted on a site created just for that purpose.

Even those who are not researching their family histories may decide to create a family-oriented website. A website incorporating your digital pictures can be a good way to share information and family news with relatives across the globe. For instance, instead of sending a yearly newsletter with your holiday cards, you could post it online and update it regularly to let visitors know all the latest news from your family. Digital photography makes it easy to show off the latest school pictures or the happy couple's wedding portrait.

Andy Warhol said that in the future everyone would be famous for 15 minutes. Every day, iWannaBeFamous *(www.iwannabefamous.com)* puts the spotlight on a person or group and makes them a star for the day by posting their photo on their website.

In conjunction with your family site, you might want to go offline to make a family tree collage using the collage tool in your image editor. Or you can gather digital images of your family, print them on high-quality paper and create a family tree by attaching them to poster board.

Developing an Online Portfolio

Artists, writers and photographers have long known the value of sharing samples of their work. Now, by creating a website and capturing his or her work digitally, an individual can create an online portfolio that is accessible to anyone with an Internet connection. Digital images can be uploaded, works of art such as drawings and paintings can be photographed with a digital camera, and printed samples can be scanned or photographed. By using an online portfolio to market your work, your services instantly become available to people you might otherwise never have met.

Glossary

adapter. A device that lets you plug a digital camera into an electrical outlet. This option is particularly useful when your batteries run out.

alkaline. A primary battery (non-rechargeable) often used in electronics, requiring heavy currents for long periods of time.

angle of view. The maximum horizontal angle seen by the lens that can be recorded on the film from edge to edge.

aperture. The opening that controls the amount of light that passes through the lens; also known as the diaphragm. The size of the aperture is measured in f-stops, which control the length of time the shutter stays open and the depth of field.

aperture priority. This mode allows the photographer to choose the aperture (controlling depth of field) while the camera sets the best matching shutter speed for desirable exposure results.

ATA. Refers to AT Attachment standards. ATA was designed as a standard interface for storage devices such as disk drives and flash memory cards for the mobile computer market. An ATA-compatible card was guaranteed to work with any system supporting ATA, including digital cameras. An ATA-compatible card also should work with all major operating systems, including Windows and Mac OS.

auto flash. A camera having an auto flash feature gauges the available light and fires the flash if needed.

autofocus. Automatically adjusts the focus depending on the distance of the subject from the camera.

backlighting. Backlighting occurs when you photograph subjects with a bright area behind them, casting them in a shadow.

balance. An even arrangement of elements in a photo.

battery charger. Replaces the charge in rechargeable batteries so that they are useable again.

bitmapping. To create an image, a computer divides the screen or printed area into a grid of pixels. Then it uses the values stored in the digital photograph to specify the brightness and colour of each pixel in the grid. This process is called bitmapping, and the resulting digital images are called bitmaps.

bottom-weighted metering. This exposure mode measures light throughout the scene but gives greater importance to the bottom of the image area.

bounce lighting. Bounce lighting refers to the technique of allowing light to bounce off the background and onto your subject, rather than aiming your light source directly at your subject.

brightness. A measurement of the light in an image; used by scanners and software.

burst mode. Some cameras offer a burst mode, which lets the photographer take photo after photo while holding down the shutter button.

camera obscura. The forerunner of today's camera, created from a darkened room or box with an opening that lets in light. The term is taken from the Latin words for 'dark room'.

centre-weighted metering. This exposure mode measures light throughout the scene but gives greater importance (weight) to the centre quarter of the image area, assuming that that is where the primary subject is located.

channel. An isolated part of the information that makes up a digital image.

charge cycle. A sequence where a charged battery is discharged and recharged.

cloning. A tool or process in an image-editing application that allows the user to 'paint' one section of an image onto another.

CMYK. Acronym for cyan, magenta, yellow and black (K represents black to prevent confusion with blue). These are the printer colours used to create colour prints. Most colour printers, including laser, inkjet, dye sublimation, thermal and crayon, use these as their printer colours.

colour balance. The process by which most digital cameras automatically adjust for the correct colour temperature; also white balance. Colour balancing determines what combination of red, green and blue light the camera should perceive as pure white under the current lighting conditions. From there, the camera determines how all other colours can be accurately represented.

colour correction. Adjusting an image to make the colours truer.

colour depth. The term used to refer to the number of colours in an image. It is also called pixel depth or bit depth.

combination scanner. A combination or multi-format scanner that scans film and slides as well as flat, printed materials.

composition. The arrangement of elements and their relationship to the background of an image.

compression. A technique used to reduce the size of an image file. It works either by reducing the number of colours in an image, or by grouping together a series of pixels of a similar colour.

condition. A process that utilizes a series of heavy discharges and recharges on a battery to assure optimum performance.

continuous mode. Allows you to snap an entire sequence of photos.

crop. This involves resizing an image so that parts of it are deleted.

curves. An adjustment command that allows the user to fine-tune brightness levels. Brightness values are shown along a curve. The user can raise or lower points on the curve to change the overall brightness of the image.

cycle life. The number of cycles under specified conditions that are available from a secondary battery before it fails to meet specified performance criteria.

daguerreotype. An early form of photography using a chemical process developed by Louis Daguerre in the 1840s.

date/time indicator. A feature of some digital cameras, the date/time indicator gives a permanent record of when the shot was taken. Some indicators are displayed in the image area, while others are hidden in the image file and can only be seen when using software.

depth of field. The measure of the area of a photograph that is in focus.

dot gain. A disadvantage of inkjet printers, dot gain occurs when ink droplets spread out when they hit the paper, causing colours to bleed into each other and images to look a little fuzzy.

download. To transfer a file from a camera to a computer or from one computer to another.

dropouts. *See* **hot spots**.

drum scanner. Uses PMT rather than CCD technology, providing greater colour accuracy. A professional wouldn't use anything but a drum scanner for producing colour separations.

dye sublimation printer. For many years, dye sublimation printers have been heralded as the top-of-the range output device for digital printing. Dye subs (for short) transfer images to paper using a plastic film or ribbon that's coated with colour dyes. During the printing process, heating elements move across the film, causing the dye to fuse to the paper. The printers work by fusing dye onto the specially manufactured transfer paper, making a separate pass through the printer for each colour.

EPS. Stands for Encapsulated PostScript. EPS files incorporate the PostScript language and the original file, so files saved in the EPS format are larger than the original. Adobe created PostScript as a means of communicating to a printer the size of the file, what fonts it uses, and other details so the printer can output an accurate document.

EXIF. Stands for Exchangeable Image Format and is a variation of the JPEG format. It was developed by the Japanese Electronics Industry Development Association.

exposure compensation. Allows the photographer to increase or decrease the exposure from what the autoexposure setting typically delivers.

fill. Lets you pour a colour, effect or texture into a closed space within an image.

fill flash. The fill flash mode allows you to add light to an image without affecting the exposure settings.

film scanner. A transparency or film scanner allows you to scan everything from a 35mm slide to a 100 x 125mm (4 x 5in) transparency. These scanners are more expensive than flatbed scanners, but they are excellent for people who want to scan a lot of transparencies as they are the only scanners that will produce quality transparency scans.

filter. An effect, such as emboss, stretch or warp, that modifies an image.

FireWire. A high-speed, high-performance serial bus. FireWire was introduced by Apple Computer in their Power Macs, but today it is used throughout the electronics industry. (FireWire is the name patented by Apple, but it is also referred to as IEEE 1394 and i.LINK.)

fixed focus. A lens with a focus that cannot be changed. Instead, the lens depends on the use of depth of field to produce sharp images.

fixed storage. Memory that cannot be increased or decreased. Once you've filled up the camera's memory, you cannot continue shooting until you've downloaded your images to a computer. Also called onboard storage.

flash. The flash provides additional lighting to the scene being photographed.

FlashPath. A type of adapter that allows you to use removable storage media with a floppy driver. It is shaped like a floppy disk and inserts into the standard drive slot found on almost all computers. You can then insert the media card into the FlashPath and begin downloading images.

FlashPix. A lossy file format that is less popular than JPEG.

flatbed scanner. A scanning device that takes its name from the flat glass platen (or bed) where you place the object to be scanned. It is very versatile and can be used to scan flat materials such as photographs and printed pages.

focal length. On film cameras, the focal length is the measurement of the distance between the centre of the lens and the film. On a digital camera, the focal length measures the distance between the lens and the image sensor. In both cases, focal length is measured in millimetres.

focus lock. Allows the photographer to centre the subject in the frame, lock the focus then reframe and take the shot. When taking a shot of a scene with many elements, this can be a useful feature because it allows you to specify which object you want to be in focus.

GIF. Another lossless compression format, GIF stands for Graphic Interchange Format.

greyscale. Refers to all shades of grey, ranging from black to white.

handheld scanner. Less expensive than a flatbed scanner and very portable, a handheld scanner is plugged directly into a computer's printer port, making it easily shared by different workstations. Often used with laptop computers.

heliography. A process developed by Joseph Niepce that is regarded as having produced the first permanent photographic image.

hot spots. Also known as dropouts, these occur when light bounces off a reflective surface and creates areas in your image that have no detail; they look like white blobs on your picture.

hot-swappable. Allows you to plug or unplug the camera from the USB port without turning off your computer or camera.

image sensors. Light-sensitive computer chips that record the image captured by a digital camera. They serve the same purpose as film in a 35mm camera.

inkjet printer. An inkjet printer works by forcing little drops of ink through nozzles onto the paper. Consumer inkjet printers have been around for many years, but they initially produced images of poor quality. Today's inkjet printers produce excellent photorealistic prints.

integrated lens. An integrated lens is part of the camera and is not detachable.

interchangeable lens. An interchangeable lens can be detached from the camera and replaced with another lens having the same type of mount.

IrDA. Wireless transfer that utilizes infrared light beams to carry files.

ISO numbers. These numbers are found on film packages and represent its speed, or sensitivity. Image sensors are also rated using ISO numbers, which are meant to be approximately equivalent to film ISOs. The lower the ISO of an image sensor, the more light that is needed for a good exposure.

ISP. Internet service provider; provides you with access to the Internet.

JPEG. An image compression method, most widely utilized by digital cameras. JPEG stands for Joint Photographic Experts Group, the people who developed the original code. Because of its ability to reduce file size with a negligible degree of deterioration, JPEG has become the standard for saving and compressing digital images.

JPEG2000. An image-coding system using state-of-the-art compression techniques, JPEG2000 provides users of digital cameras with a more versatile JPEG file format that uses wavelet technology. It represents a significant advancement in image-compression technology.

laser printer. A laser printer uses a technology similar to photocopiers; a laser beam produces electrical charges on a drum inside the printer. The drum then rolls ink onto the paper, and heat is applied, which permanently affixes the toner to the page.

layering. Stacking elements in an image. The layering tool lets you edit elements such as images, graphics and text separately from each other. You also can change the settings, colouration, effects and many more variables for each layer.

lens. An optical glass or plastic element used to gather and focus rays of light and form an image.

lens cap. A lens cap protects a camera's lens. It is especially important for digital cameras, which are particularly susceptible to scratching and smearing because the cameras are so small that your fingers may end up on top of the lens.

lens hood. A lens hood, or lens shade, hinders unwanted light from striking the lens. It also affords your lens some protection from knocks and bumps.

light-balancing filter. A filter that compensates for different lighting conditions.

line. Shapes are defined by lines. As we view a photo, our eyes follow its lines. One of the most important uses of line is to lead the viewer to the centre of interest in a photograph.

lithium ion (Li-Ion). One of the newer and more expensive rechargeable battery technologies, Li-Ion batteries can deliver more capacity than comparably sized NiCad batteries and are among the lightest rechargeable batteries available today.

macro lens. Allows you to focus while standing very close to your subject in order to take close-up shots.

magnification. Magnification goes hand-in-hand with angle of view. A short lens, with its wide angle of view, requires all the objects in a scene to be reduced in size in order to fit into the image sensor, and has the effect of pushing the subject away from you. Conversely, the long lens, with its corresponding narrow angle of view, will have the effect of pulling objects in a scene close to you, causing them to appear larger.

masking. The masking tool preserves areas of an image. Masking permits you to apply an effect to one specific part of an image or to vary the strength of an effect within an image.

matrix metering. The default autoexposure mode on a digital camera, matrix metering, also called multizone metering, works by dividing the frame into a grid, or matrix. Then it analyzes light at different points on the grid and chooses an exposure that best captures both the dark and light sections of the scene.

megapixel. Used to describe the resolution that can be produced by a digital camera's image sensor; indicates that there are millions of pixels in the image.

nickel cadmium (NiCad) battery. NiCad batteries are the most widely used type of rechargeable household battery and are used in small, portable devices such as cameras, radios, laptop computers and mobile phones. A dependable and popular rechargeable battery, NiCad has a relatively low capacity when compared to other rechargeable systems. Contains cadmium, which is toxic.

nickel metal hydride (NiMH) battery. Interchangeable with most NiCad batteries, nickel metal hydride (NiMH) batteries generally deliver greater capacity than NiCads. NiMH batteries are the most popular batteries for digital camera use because they are rechargeable, nontoxic and relatively inexpensive.

night flash. Night flash, or night portrait mode, combines a flash exposure with a longer capture speed. This mode is ideal for shooting room lights or an evening sky with a brightly lit subject.

noise. Small imperfections that can ruin a perfectly good photograph. Noise comes from the light sensors in your camera, resulting in an image that appears grainy or snowy, similar to a snowy image on a TV screen or a grainy film photograph. Noise tends to appear when a too-high ISO rating is chosen, or when using image-editing software to correct an underexposed area.

parallel port. Parallel ports are normally used for printers and certain kinds of external storage devices, and they carry 8 bits of data at a time. Many card readers plug into a parallel port.

path. A path shows the area where an effect will be applied in an image-editing application. It is shown as a border around an object.

pattern. The repetition of lines, shapes or colours. Patterns have strong visual impact, and even the suggestion of a pattern in a photo can catch the viewer's eye.

PC Cards. Also called PCMCIA (Personal Computer Memory Card International Association) cards; a type of removable memory card.

PDF. An updated version of the EPS format, PDF (portable document format) also contains information that is helpful to the printer, including descriptions of font, size and colour.

photography. The process of recording an image on a sensitive material. The term was coined by Sir John Herschel in 1839 from the Greek words for light (*photos*) and drawing (*graphein*).

photorealistic print. A print made from a digitized photo, as opposed to a 'photograph', which is a conventional picture printed in a darkroom.

pixel. The basic element of resolution. Derived from 'picture element' or 'picture cell'.

plug-in. Software that expands an established software program by providing an added feature. With plug-ins, you'll gain more features for your software without having to spend a lot on upgrading. Free plug-ins on CD-ROMs are sometimes given away with magazines.

polarizing filter. A filter that removes glare caused by reflected light and tends to improve colour saturation.

previsualization. The ability to imagine while shooting how the resulting photo will look.

primary battery. A battery that is not intended to be recharged and is discarded when it has delivered all its electrical energy.

rechargeable battery. A battery that can be recharged and used again and again.

red-eye. The red-eye effect occurs when a flash is reflected in the subject's eyes.

resampling. A process that deletes or blends pixels in order to reduce an image's resolution without changing its width and height. Resampling can help reduce the size of files used on a website so that they download faster.

resolution. A measure of the amount of detail that an image possesses.

RGB. Red, green and blue; the primary colours for transmitted light. Computer monitors, TVs and digital cameras display their pixels based on values of red, green and blue. When mixed together, red, green and blue create white light.

rule of thirds. A formula for achieving balance, which requires that the photographer mentally divides an image into thirds, both horizontally and vertically. For instance, subjects are placed near one of the four intersections to provide immediate off-centre emphasis, or placed at diagonally opposed intersections to create a balanced composition.

saturation. The intensity of a colour. Image-editing software allows the user to boost or reduce saturation as needed.

SCSI. Stands for Small Computer System Interface; transfers data at a rate of from 40Mbps (megabits per second) to 640Mbps, making it up to 50 times faster than a USB connection. Historically used by Macintosh computers, SCSI is fast, but it does have certain drawbacks, so USB is used more widely.

secondary battery. A battery that can be recharged and reused many times (rechargeable battery).

selection. The specified section of an image to which an effect will be applied.

self-timer. A mechanism that delays the shutter release for about ten seconds, allowing you to get into a picture before the shutter releases. This is a useful feature when you want to take a self-portrait or include yourself in a group shot.

serial port. Generally used for connecting analogue modems so that the user can access the Internet. Some digital cameras still use serial ports to connect to a computer. A serial cable

transmits information one bit of data at a time, which makes for a very slow process.

shape. The first thing our eyes distinguish when looking at a photograph.

shutter priority. This mode allows the photographer to choose the shutter speed, and the camera then sets the best matching aperture.

slave unit. A slave unit is a small, battery-operated flash unit with built-in photo eyes. The slave unit fires a flash when it senses another flash of light.

slow-sync flash. Some cameras offer a slow-sync flash, which increases the exposure time beyond the normal flash. This mode helps illuminate background shadows that normal flash mode misses. The slow-synchronized mode works by allowing the shutter to remain open longer than normal so that the background appears lighter.

SLR. Single-lens reflex; a type of camera that uses one lens for both shooting and viewing. Allows the photographer to see exactly what the camera sees.

small-footprint scanner. A smaller, lighter and more durable scanner than its CCD-based counterparts; ideal for taking on the road or fitting into cramped spaces such as spare rooms.

solid inkjet printer. A solid inkjet printer uses sticks of crayon-like ink that are heated and dropped onto the paper.

spot metering. This exposure mode measures the light only at the centre of the image.

spot reading. A technique for combatting back-lighting, spot reading enables the photographer to take a reading in a smaller area, such as the shaded area of the subject. Once the spot reading is complete, the camera automatically opens the aperture, creating an image that is properly exposed.

SRAM. Static RAM technology that holds data without electric current. Flash memory cards use SRAM.

texture. Adds a sense of realism to a photo and appeals to the viewer's sense of touch.

thermo-autochrome printer. Uses thermal wax to heat pigment-carrying wax from a print ribbon. Thermo-autochrome printers are faster than dye sublimation printers because they use sticks of wax or ribbons of dye rather than ink cartridges. The technique is similar to that seen on fax machines that print on thermal paper.

TIFF. An acronym for Tagged Image File Format, this format allows you to store the highest-quality uncompressed images. It is the most popular loss-less compression format.

tolerance. A setting that determines how discrim-inating a selection tool will be in matching the criteria you specify.

transparency. An effect that changes the opacity of an element so that underlying elements can show through.

unsharp masking. A sharpening filter frequently used to regain sharpness lost in the scanning process.

upload. To transfer a file from a computer to a camera.

URL. Uniform resource locator; the 'address' or location of a website or other Internet service.

USB. Universal serial bus; a type of connection found on the majority of modern computers. Downloading via the USB is a much faster and easier way to transfer your images than using a serial cable. USB can transfer images at up to 12Mbps, which is about 50 times as fast as the fastest serial connection. In addition to saving you time when you download, another great advantage to using a USB camera is it's hot-swappable, so you don't have to turn off the computer or the camera when you plug or unplug the camera from the USB port. With USB, you can 'daisy chain' up to 127 devices on a single USB port, which makes it easy to custom-build a system. You can use USB with CD-ROM drives, hard drives and video equipment.

UV filter. A UV (ultraviolet) filter removes ultra-violet light, which commonly shows up in the background of distant shots as a bluish haze.

vector images. Shapes defined using the mathe-matical principle of vectors. Digital drawings are vector images. Some software programs let the user draw well-defined vector images of various shapes.

white balance. *See* **colour balance**.

zoom lens. A zoom lens has a variable focal length, meaning it allows you to adjust the focal length over a variety of ranges.

Resources

Camera Manufacturer Websites

Every major camera manufacturer has a website. Although you may not be able to purchase online, you will find lots of information on the various models they offer, including specifications, photos and press releases.

Agfa
www.agfanet.com
Argus
www.arguscamera.com
Bronica
www.tamron.com
Canon
www.canon.com
Casio
www.casio.com
Epson
www.epson.com
Fuji
www.fujifilmcom
JVC
www.jvc.com
Kodak
www.kodak.com
Konica
www.konica.com
Leica
www.leica.com
Minolta
www.minolta.com

Nikon
www.nikon.com
Olympus
www.olympus.com
Panasonic
www.panasonic.com
Pentax Corp.
www.pentax.com
Polaroid
www.polaroid.com
Ricoh
www.ricoh.com
Samsung
www.samsung.com
Sanyo
www.sanyodigital.com
Sharp
www.sharp.com
Sony
www.sony.com
Vivitar
www.vivitar.com

Scanner Manufacturer Websites

Here are some manufacturer websites you may want to explore to see what types of scanners are available.

Agfa
www.agfa.com
Canon
www.canon.com
Epson
www.epson.com
Fuji
www.fujifilm.com
Hewlett-Packard
www.hp.com
Kodak
www.kodak.com
Konica
www.konica.com

LinoColor
www.heidelberg.com
Mustek
www.mustekdirect.com
Nikon
www.nikon.com
Plustek
www.plustekusa.com
Umax
www.umax.com
Visioneer
www.visioneer.com

Index

Page numbers in italics refer to photographs.

A

ACD*See* file manager, 172, 173
Acer, 176
Action shots, 127, 201. *See also* Photography
ActionTec, 59
Adams, Ansel, 105, 113, 134–35, 137, 138
Adaptec, 147
ADC (analogue-to-digital converter), 183
Adobe, 161, 175, 193, 230, 233–34
Aladdin Systems, 164
Alkaline batteries, 84
analog-to-digital converter (ADC), 183
Angle of view, 64, *112*, 112–13
Animated photography, 100
Aperture, 19, 66
Aperture priority mode, 95, 97–98
Apple Computers, 101, 148, 149
APS (Advanced Photo System) cameras, 34
Archive formats, 162–64
ArcSoft, 236
Aristotle, 3
Artistic effects, 217
Aspect ratio, 50–51
ATA-compatible cards, 58
ATA standards, 58
Autoexposure, 94–95
Autoflash, 76–77, 98
Autofocus lens, 67–68, 98
Aware Inc., 159

B

Background, refining, 211
Backlighting, 76–77, 81, 82, 96, 116

Balance, *110*, 110–11
Balancing filters, 72
Barbaro, Daniel, 3
Batteries
    buying on the Web, 88–89
    caution on, 85
    chargers for, 31, 32, 86, 88
    draining, 83, 146
    prolonging life, 88
    prolonging life of, 12
    ratings, 86
    ready to use, 87
    removing, 45
    trickle charge, 86
    types of, 84–86
Battista della Porta, Giovanni, 2
Bell Laboratories, 49
bin Hassan, Hassan, 3
Binary digits, 20
Bit depth, 20, 51
Bitberry Software, 163
Bitmaps, 20, 50
Bits, 20, 180–81
Bits per pixel, 20
BitZipper compression utility, 163–64
Black-and-white photos, 219
Blooming, 48, 49
Blurring
    avoiding, 120
    creative use of, 78
    fixed focus and, 67
    image-editing software, 216
    reflections and, 70
    slow-sync mode and, 78
BMP formats, 162
Body housing, 19
Borders, 223
Bottom-weighted metering, 96
Boyle, Robert, 3
Bracketing, 97
Brightening images, 214

Brightness value, 18
Broderbund, 222
Brownie camera, 7, 67
Bubble-jet printers, 193
Burning CDs, 169, 170
Burning images, 214
Burst mode, 52
Business owners, and digital photography, 224–25
Bytes, 20

C

Cable release
    for night shots, 82
    for steady shots, 120
Calendars
    from digital images, 223
Calotype, 4
Camera bags, 44–45
Camera costs, 33–34
Camera manuals, 119, 120
Camera manufacturer websites, 251
Camera obscura, 3
Camera phones, 152
Camera types, 33–34
Cameron, Julia Margaret, 5
Canon, 73, 149, 177, 191, 193
Canon EOS D30, 49
Canon Optura Pi, 35
Cartier-Bresson, Henri, 127, 132
Casio, 151
CCD chips
    CIS technology and, 183
    CMOS chips and, 48–49, 179
    light sensitivity and, 16–17, 81
    manufacturing of, 47
    resolution and, 33
CD-R (CD-Recordable) drives, 169
CD-ROM drives, 167, 169
CD-RW (CD-Rewritable) drives, 169

CDs, 167, 169, 170
Centre-weighted metering, 96
Charge-coupled device chips. *See* CCD chips
Chargers, 32, 146
Chemical process, 4
Children, and digital photography, 222–23
Chips, 16
CIS technology, 179, 183
Cleaning kit
    for cameras, 45
    for lenses, 65
Click-to-click rate, 51–52
ClickArt 300,000 Premier Image Pak, 222
Cloning tool, 204, 207
Close-up mode, 71, 141–42
Close-ups, 68, 70–72, 141–42, 200
Cloudy settings, 100
CMOS APS, 49
CMOS chips
    CCD chips and, 48–49, 179
    light sensitivity and, 16–17
    manufacturing of, 47
    resolution and, 33
CMYK colours, 178, 190
Cold protection, 45–46
Collages, 218
Colour
    balance of, 72–73, 99–100
    changing, 219
    correcting, 209, 214
    depth of, 51
    manipulating, 114
    mood and, 113–14
    quality of, 12, 18
Colour laser printers, 193
Colour photograph reference, 118
Colour separations, 178
Colour temperature filters, 72–73, 99
Combination scanners, 177

Commercial photography, 13, 224–25
CompactFlash cards
    downloading images, 148, 150–51
    durability of, 57
    memory capacity, 31, 34
    memory card readers, 60
    printers and, 154
    removable memory, 30
    types of, 58–59
Compaq, 149
Complementary metal-oxide semiconductor chips. *See* CMOS chips
Composites, 218
Composition, *109*, 109–10
Compression formats, 162–64
Compression mode, 30, 53
CompuServe, 160
Computer connections, 31, 32, 146–49
Computer-free printing, 194
Computer software. *See also* Image-editing software
    types of, 32
Condensation, 46
Contact image sensor (CIS) technology, 179, 183
Continuous mode, 100, 201
Contouring filter, 217
Contrasting colours, 114
Contrasting images, 214
Controls, 93–102
Converging verticals, 209–10
Cool colours, 113–14
Copier paper, 197
Corel, 231–32, 235
Creative controls, 93–102
Cropping images, 214

D
da Vinci, Leonardo, 2
Daguerre, Louis, 4
Daguerreotypes, 4–6

Damp photo shoots, 45
Darkening images, 214
Darkening photos, 96–97
Darkroom techniques, 202, 213
Darkrooms, 3
DataPlay, 61
Date/time indicator, 101
Daylight settings, 100
Delays, 51–52
Depth, creating, 105
Digital cameras
    accessories for, 44–45
    benefits of, 7–11
    budget for, 33, 38
    caring for, 44–46
    cost of, 11–12, 32–34
    disadvantages of, 8–9, 11–12
    elements of, 16–17
    evaluating, 32
    hiring, 29
    meeting needs, 28–31, 34–36, 38–39
    purchasing, 43–44
    purchasing online, 42–43,
    researching, 39–42
    selecting, 28–36, 38–46
    technology and, 44, 56
    websites about, 40–41
Digital darkroom
    capabilities, 214–15
    techniques, 202, 213
    tools for, 203–5
Digital Flash system, 79
Digital images. *See* Images
Digital photo albums, 224–25, 228, 239–41
Digital photography. *See also* Photography
    commercial uses for, 13, 224–25
    magazines on, 41–42
Digital portfolios, 240–41
Digital versatile disk (DVD), 171
Digital video cameras, 34

Digital videos, 9. *See also* Slide shows
Digital zoom lens, 69
Dimensions, of image, 20
Disk adapters, 60
Distortion, 218–19
Dodging images, 214
Dots per inch (dpi), 24, 175–76
Downloading images, 145–54
Downsampling, 22
dpi (dots per inch), 24, 175–76
DPOF (digital print order format), 194
Drum scanners, 178
Duotones, 214
DVDs (digital versatile disks), 171
DVD-Rs, 171
DVD-RAMs, 171
DVD-ROMs, 171
Dye sublimation printers, 191–92

E
E-mailing images, 238–39
Eastman American Film, 6
Eastman Dry Plat and Film Company, 6
Eastman, George, 6
Eastman Kodak Company, 6, 152
eBay, 42
Edge softening tool, 208
Edison, Thomas, 7
(e)film, 12
eFilm, 58, 59
eFilm Pocket Reader, 60
Einstein, Albert, 122
Electronic film cartridge, 12
Enroute Imaging, 101
EPS format, 161, 195
Epson, 152, 197, 202
EXIF format, 160
Exposure, 80
Exposure compensation, 96–98
Exposure value (EV), 96
External flash, 78

Eyemodule2, 35, 36

F
F-stops, 66
Fairchild Semiconductor, 44
Fast-action shots, 51
File compression, 30, 53, 155–64
File formats
    proprietary, 162
    for storage, 167
    types of, 157–62, 204
Film, 7–9
Film format chart, 65
Film scanners, 176–77
Film sensitivity, 52
Film speed, 52, 81
Filters, 65, 72, 99, 216, 217, 221
FilZip compression utility, 163
FireReaders, 148
FireWire, 148–49, 150, 168
FireWireDirect, 148
Fixed-focus lens, 67, 98
Flash, 75–82
    adding, 76, 78, 79
    auto mode, 76–77, 98
    built-in, 52, 76, 79
    external unit, 78
    fill mode, 77
    light sources and, 77, 79–82
    limitations of, 76
    memory for, 57–59
    night portrait mode, 77
    red-eye reduction, 77–78, 79
    settings for, 76, 100
    slow-sync mode, 78
FlashPath adapter, 149
FlashPix (FPX) format, 161–62
Flatbed scanners, 174, 175–76
Floppy disks, 149, 169
Floppy drives, 169
Fluorescent settings, 100
Focal length
    changing, 64
    determining, 65
    zoom lens and, 69

Focus lock, 98–99
Focusing
    distances, 68, 98–99
    image-editing software, 216
    methods, 66–68
Frame rate, 32, 51–52
Frames, 223
Framing, 113
Freeware, 172
Frontlighting, 116

G
Genealogy website, 240
Giant Camera, 3
GIF format, 160–61, 186
Gifts
    from digital images, 223–24
Glowing edges filter, 221
Greetings cards
    from digital images, 223
Grey cards, 80
Group f/64, 138

H
Halos, 48
Hand-colouring images, 214
Handheld computer cameras, 35
Handheld digital video cameras, 35
Handheld scanners, 178–79
Handspring Visor, 35
Hard drives, 168
Heat protection, 45
Heliography, 3
Herschel, Sir John, 3
Hewlett-Packard, 152, 161
Highlights, capturing, 49
Hitachi Maxell Ltd., 60
Hoodman Corporation, 91
Horizon line, *111*, 112, 135
Horizontal formats, 209
Host-based printing, 194
Hot shoe, 76, 79
Hot-swappable capabilities, 148

I

IBM, 60
iD PHOTO media, 60
IDC-1000Z iDshot, 60
IEEE 1394, 148
i.LINK, 148
Image-editing software, 227–36
  advanced programs, 228,
    230–32
  artistic effects, 217–18
  beginner programs, 234–35
  choosing, 202–3, 228–30
  cost of, 202–3
  ease of use, 204–5
  features of, 209
  fun with, 222–24
  intermediate programs,
    232–34
  for manipulating images, 159, 185
  overview of, 232
  for red-eye reduction, 78, 204, 210
  resampling and, 22
  resizing and, 23
  special effects, 207–8, 218–22
  tips on, 206
  tools for, 203–6, 217
  trial versions, 230
  for Web images, 205
Image sensors
  aspect ratio, 50–51
  capturing images, 55
  CCD chips, 16–17, 47–50
  CIS technology, 179, 183
  CMOS chips, 16–17, 47–50
  resolutions, 50
  sensitivity of, 52–53
Image storage, 55–61. *See also*
  Storage devices
ImageMate Drive, 150–51
Imagepower, 159
Images
  adding text, 219
  adjusting, 22–24
  capturing, 16, 200–1

combining, 210
commercial uses for, 13,
  224–26
correcting, 208–11
downloading, 145–54
duplicating, 206–7
e-mailing, 238–39
experimenting with, 211,
  222–24
layering, 203
life of, 11, 198
manipulating, 159, 203, 208,
  214–15
mirroring, 221
printing, 21
quality of, 7, 11–12, 24–25, 53
refining, 211
resizing, 23, 25
sharpening, 210
size of, 20, 22, 25, 53
storing, 165–71
tips for, 126
transferring, 30, 146–48,
  151–52
use of, 21
on websites, 21, 22, 237–42
Imaging tools, 203–6, 217
Imbalance, 110–11
Incandescent settings, 100
Infrared effects, 220, *220*
Infrared transfers, 151–52
Inkjet paper, 201
Inkjet printers, 190–91, 196
Inspiration, 120
Integrated lenses, 68
Intel Corporation, 44
Interchangeable lenses, 68, 72
Interpolation, 22
Inverting images, 214
Iomega, 31, 151, 170, 171
IrDA (wireless infrared), 151–52
ISO (International Organization
  for Standardization) ratings,
  52–53, 81

IWannaBeFamous.com, 240

J

Japanese Electronics Industry
  Development Association, 160
Jasc Software, 234
Jaz drives, 169
Joint Photographic Experts
  Group (JPEG). *See* JPEG
  format
JPEG format, 53, 100, 157–58,
  160, 162, 186
JPEG2000 (JP2) format, 158–59
JPL (Jet Propulsion Laboratory), 49

K

Kodak, 149, 151, 152, 161
Kodak Camera, 6
Kodak PalmPix, 36
Kodak Personal Picture Maker
  200, 194
Kodak PhotoNet Online, 252
Kratochwilz, Franz, 6

L

Landscape mode, 68, 209
Laser printers, 193
Layering tool, 203
LCD screens
  example of, *89*
  hood for, 91
  previewing shots with, 96, 97,
    122
  tips on, 32, 33, 90, 92
Leibovitz, Annie, 131
Lenses, 19, 63–74
  accessories for, 72–74
  angle of view, 64
  aperture of, 66
  autofocus, 67–68
  caps for, 73
  cleaning, 65
  composition of, 63, 70
  evaluating, 73–74
  filters for, 65, 72

fixed focus, 67
focal length of, 64–65
hoods for, 73
magnification, 64
manual focus, 67
maximum aperture of, 66
protecting, 73
speed of, 66
types of, 64–65, 68–72, *70*, 74
Lexar Media, 58
Lexmark, 194
Life, 120
Light
  effects on photos, 115
  colour and, 18
  from the sun, 115
Light filters, 72
Light intensity, 18, 66
Light meters, 95
Light sensitivity, 48, 49, 81,
  114–17
Light sensors, 48
Light sources
  backlighting, 81–82
  controlling, 80
  film speed and, 81
  placement of, 80
  slave unit, 79–80
Lightening photos, 96–97, 214
Li-Ion (lithium ion) batteries,
  85–86
Lines, 104–6, *105*, *124*
Lithographic effects, 219
Live Picture, 161
Long lens, 64, 65
Long-term shooting, 31
Looney Tunes PhotoFun, 223
Lossless compression, 156–57
Lossy compression, 157
Loupe, 190

M

Macintosh computers, 147, 164,
  170
Macro lenses, 70–71

Macro mode, 68
Macro photography, 71–72
Magazines on digital photog-
  raphy, 41–42
Magic Series, 228
Magnetic fields, 45
Magnetic media, 167, 168–69
Magnification, 64
Manual focus lens, 67
Manuals, for cameras, 119, 120
Masking images, 215
Matrix metering, 96
Maximum aperture, 66
Megapixel resolution, 23, 28–29
Memorable photographs,
  103–17
Memory
  large files and, 22, 25
  removable memory, 29–31,
    55–61
  types of, 166
Memory cards
  capacity of, 31
  caring for, 61
  formatting, 61
  PC cards, 57–58
  readers, 59–60, 146–48, 150
  removable memory, 29–31,
    55–61
  types of, 57–59
Metering system, 95–96
MGI Software, 223, 236
Microdrive cards, 60
Microsoft Corporation, 161, 170,
  235
Minds@Work, 60
Minolta, 152
Mirror images, 221
Monitors, 23–24
Monochromatic photos, 219
Montages, 218
Moore, Gordon, 44
Moore's Law, 44
Mosaic filter, 217

Motion picture camera, 7
Motorola, 152
Movement, 110

N

NASA Jet Propulsion Laboratory
  (JPL), 49
Native formats, 162, 186
Natural Magic, 2
Negatives, 4, 11
Neutral density filters, 72
NiCad (nickel cadmium) bat-
  teries, 85
Niepce, Joseph, 3–4
Night flash, 77
Night photography, 77, 82
Nikon, 73, 149, 177, 185
NiMH (nickel metal hydride)
  batteries, 84–85
Noise problems, 48, 53
Normal lens, 64, 65
Novelty items
  from digital images, 223–24

O

O'Keeffe, Georgia, 137
OCR (optical character recogni-
  tion) software, 175, 185
OD (optical density), 176, 183
Office Depot, 185
Oil painting filter, 217
Olympus Optical Co., Ltd., 60, 73
Onboard memory, 29–30
Online auctions, 42–43
Online photo album, 239–41
Online portfolios, 240–41
Online resources, 241
Online storage services, 172
Onscreen displays
  image size, 22, 239
  resolution for, 21, 25, 28
Optical media, 167, 169–70
Optical process, 3
Optical zoom lens, 69
Overcast settings, 100

P

Paint Shop Pro, 175, 234
Painting tools, 217
Paintings, from photographs, 217
Palette knife filter, 217
Panoramic mode, 101, 135
Papers, for printers, 197–98
Parallax error, 91–92
Parallel ports, 147, 184
Patterns, 106–7
  examples of, *106, 107*
  manipulating, 220–21
PC cards
  adapters for, *59*, 150
  types of, 57–58
PC805 PC Card Reader, 59
PCMCIA cards, 57
PDAs (personal digital assistants), 35
PDD format, 162
PDF format, 161
Perspective, 105
Petzval, Jozsef, 6
Photo Paint, 231–32
Photo Paint 9 Digital Camera Edition, 235
Photo printing, 196. *See also* Printers; Printing
PhotoAlbum 3, 225
PhotoAlbum Studio, 225
PhotoDeluxe, 162
Photoflood lights, 80
Photographers
  professional fields, 13, 33–34, 48–49
  tips for, 119–28
Photographic paper, 197
Photographic process, 3–5
Photographs
  albums for, 224–25, 228, 239–41
  building blocks of, 103–17
  composition of, 200

  improving, 199–211
  tips on, 119–28, 126
  types of, 129–42
Photography
  action shots, 127, 201
  animation, 100
  architectural details, *140, 140–41, 141*
  bracketing, 97
  candid shots, 131–32
  children and, 222–23
  city scenes, 138–40
  city skylines, 64, 101, 139
  close-ups, 68, 70–72, 141–42, 200
  coastline scenes, 101, *134*
  decisive moments, 126–27, *127*, 132
  definition of, 3
  details, 126
  fast-action shots, 51
  fluorescent scenarios, 100
  fun with, 224–26
  group shots, 102, 201
  hobbies and, 123
  landscapes, 64, 133–36, *134–35*
  nature scenes, 64
  night shots, 77, 82
  overcast scenarios, 100
  panoramic scenes, 101, 135–36
  pets, 132–33
  portraits, 64, 124, *125*, 130–31, 201–2
  previewing shots, 96, 97, 122
  recording events, 123–24
  recording information, 143
  shady scenes, 95
  silhouettes, 138, 222
  still life shots, 136–38
  sunny scenes, 95, 100, 115
  sunsets, 136
  taking great pictures, 119–28
  time and nature, 127–28
  time and people, 128
  weather effects on, *116*, 117

Photography log, 143
PhotoImpact, 205, 233
PhotoParade Maker, 228–29
Photorealistic prints, 189, 190
Photoshop
  cost of, 204, 231
  file format, 162
  sophistication of, 228
  tips on, 227
Photoshop Elements, 233–34
Photosites, 17, 50
PhotoStudio 5.5, 236
PhotoSuite, 236
Physical dimensions, 20
PICT formats, 162
Picture cell, 18
Picture element, 18
Picture It!, 235
Picture-taking tips, 119–28
Pixel count, 20
Pixel depth, 51
Pixel dimensions, 20, 23
Pixelization, 19, *19*
Pixels
  adding, 22
  adjusting, 22–24
  creating images, 50
  deleting, 22
  explanation of, 18
  number needed, 21
  resolution and, 20–21
Pixels per inch (ppi)
  changing, 22
  dpi and, 24
  explanation of, 20
  monitors and, 23–24
  resolution and, 20–21, 25
Plastic bags, for camera, 45, 46
Platform-specific formats, 162
Plug-ins, 278
PMT (Photo Multiplier Tube) technology, 178
PNG, 160
Pocket Kodak Camera, 7

PocketZip, 31, 151
Pointillist filter, 217
Polarizing filters, 72
Polaroid, 176
Portfolios, online, 240–41
Portrait mode, 68, 209
Positives, 4, 11
Posterization, 215
Postscript printing, 195
PowerShot S300 Digital Elph, 65
ppi (pixels per inch). *See* Pixels per inch
Previewing shots, 96, 97, 122
Previsualization, 123, 134
Printers, 189–98
  cartridges, 196–97
  choosing, 193–94
  cost of, 190, 191, 193
  hookups for, 32
  interfaces, 196
  paper types, 197–98
  resolution of, 24, 195
  toners, 196–97
  types of, 190–93
  warranties, 197
Printing
  images, 21, 34, 154
  photos, 196
  process of, 190
  types of, 194–95
Prints
  life of, 11, 198
Proprietary formats, 162, 186
PSD format, 162

Q
QPS Inc., 168
QuickStitch, 101
QuickTime, 101

R
RAM (random access memory)
  large files and, 22, 25
  memory cards and, 29–30
  types of, 166

Rechargeable batteries, 31, 84–86
Recording events, 123–24
Recycle time, 52
Red-eye reduction, 77–78, 79, 130, 204, 210
Reflections, 221
Refresh rate, 51
Remote controls, 102
Removable memory, 29–31, 55–61
Resampling, 22
Resizing, 23, 25
Resolution
  adjusting, 22–24
  of cameras, 23
  chips and, 17
  measuring, 20, 25
  meeting needs, 28–29
  of monitors, 23–24
  pixels and, 20–21
  of printers, 21, 24
  quality of, 12, 18–21, 25
  of scanners, 24, 181–82
  for websites, 21, 25, 28
Reticulation, 215
Retouching images, 215
Reynolds, Joshua, 2
RGB images, 18
Rim lighting, 116
Ripple filter, 221
Rosenberg, Ron, 57
Rubber stamp tool, 204
Rule of thirds, *111*, 111–12

S
Sabbatier effect, 215
Sandby, Paul, 2
SanMate, 150
Scanners, 173–88
  bit depth, 180–815
  caring for, 186
  choosing, 181–86
  colour depth, 182–83
  cost of, 181
  density range, 183
  extras, 185–86

  interfaces, 184
  resolution of, 24, 181–82
  software, 184–85
  specifications, 180, 182
  speed of, 183–84
  three-dimensional objects, 174–75
  tips on scanning, 187
  tools for, 186
  types of, 175–79
  uses for, 173, 181
ScanSoft, 174
Schulze, Johann Heinrich, 3
SCSI ports, 147, 184
Secure Digital cards
  downloading images, 148, 150–51
  editing images, 174
  memory capacity, 31, 34
  memory card readers, 60
  printers and, 154
  removable memory, 30
  transferring images, 172, 173
  types of, 58–59
Self-timer
  for night shots, 82
  for self-portraits, 102
Sensitivity of film, 52
Serial ports, 146–47
Settings, 76, 100
Shapes, 104, *104*
Sharp, 151
Sharpness, improving, 210
Short lens, 64, 65
Shot-to-shot rate, 51–52
Shots. *See* Photography
Shutter, 19
Shutter lag, 201
Shutter priority mode, 95, 97–98
Sidelighting, 116
Silhouetting, 138, 224
Silicon Film Technologies, Inc., 12
Slave unit, 79–80

Slide shows, 225, 241. *See also* Digital videos

Slow-sync flash, 78

SLR (single-lens-reflex) cameras, 12, 19, 34

Small-footprint scanners, 179

SmartDisk, 59

Softening tool, 207

Software. *See also* Image-editing software
types of, 32

Solarization, 215

Solid inkjet printers, 192–93

Sony, 149, 151, 169

Special effects, 207–08, 218–22

Speciality papers, 197

Speed of film, 52, 81

Speed of lenses, 66

Sponging images, 214

Spot metering, 96

SRAM (static RAM), 57

Stationery
from digital images, 223

Steichen, Edward, 142

Stieglitz, Alfred, 137

Stitching software, 101, 136

Stock photographs, 218

Storage devices. *See also* Image storage
downloading from, 149–51
online, 172
types of, 167–71

Strand, Paul, 137

Studio lights, 80

StuffIt Deluxe, 164

Sunpak, 79

Super floppies, 168

SuperJPG, 174–75

T

T-shirts
from digital images, 223

Talbot, William Henry Fox, 4

Technological advances, 44, 56

Telephoto lenses, 64, 65, 74

Television connections, 153–54

Text, adding to images, 219

Texture, *108*, 108–9

Thermo-autochrome printers, 192

Thumbnail images, 146

TIFF format, 159–60, 162, 186

Tile filter, 217

Time-lapse photography, 100

TimePix, 120

Toshiba, 61

Transfer cable, 146

Transfer speeds, 146–48

Tripod
for night shots, 82
for reducing blurring, 78
for steady shots, 120

Tungsten settings, 100

Turtle, Gene, 3

Twirl filter, 221

U

Ulead, 233

UMAX, 179

Unbundling, 39

Underexposure, 81

Universal serial bus (USB) port, 31, 32

Upsampling, 22

USB ports
for digital cameras, 31, 32, 60
for downloads, 147–48
for printers, 196
for scanners, 184

UV filters, 65, 72

V

Vaporware, 176

VCR connections, 153–54

Vector Flash Memory Reader, 59

Vermeer, Johannes, 2

Vertical formats, 209

VGA (video graphics array), 23

Video cameras, 34, 35

Video recording mode, 100

Viewfinders, 90–92

Vignetting, 222

Voigtlander, Friedrich, 6

W

Warhol, Andy, 240

Warm colours, 113–14

Warping, 218–19

Watercolour filter, 217

Wavelet technology, 158–59

Webcams, 35

Websites
about digital cameras, 40–41
of auctions, 42–43
for batteries, 88–89
of camera manufacturers, 251
file formats for, 158–60
image size for, 22, 239
photo albums for, 240
of photo contests, 142
resolution for, 21, 25, 28
of scanner manufacturers, 252

Wegman, William, 133

Weston, Edward, 137–38

Wet photo shoots, 45

White balance, 99

Wide-angle lenses, 64, 65, 74

WinZip compression utility, 163

Wireless transfers, 151–52

Wolcott, Alexander, 6

Workshops, 120–21

X

xD-Picture Card, 56

XGA (extended graphics array), 23

Z

ZDNet, 185

Zip drives, 168

Zip files, 162–64

Zone System, 134–35

Zoom lenses, 69, *70*, 74